Y LDS

NOTES OF
A FILM DIRECTOR

SERGEI EISENSTEIN

With a Note by RICHARD GRIFFITH,
Curator Emeritus, The Museum of
Modern Art Film Library

DOVER PUBLICATIONS, INC.
NEW YORK

This Dover edition, first published in 1970, is a
corrected republication of the English translation
(by X. Danko) of *Zamyetki Kinoryezhissyora*
(compiled and edited by R. Yurenev), originally
issued by the Foreign Languages Publishing
House, Moscow, n.d. [after 1948]. It is unabridged
except for one page of unessential material considered unsuitable for reprinting. A new prefatory
note has been written specially for this edition by
Richard Griffith, and a list of illustrations has been
added. The present edition also includes 14 additional stills and photographs, some never before
published, used by courtesy of The Museum of
Modern Art/Film Stills Archive.

International Standard Book Number: 0–486–22392–2
Library of Congress Catalog Card Number: 70–83718

NOTE TO THE DOVER EDITION

From the time of *Potemkin* until his death, S. M. Eisenstein poured forth a stream of critical and theoretical articles, short and long. They were mostly short because they were produced under pressure or in response to stimuli external to Eisenstein's own work and thought—his lifelong "interior monologue." Some were written at the invitation of foreign lovers of his work, and thus were consciously addressed to the readership of European or American film journals. Others, published first or exclusively in the Soviet Union, were responses to Soviet political developments or to the internal politics of the Soviet film industry, which Eisenstein conceived as an unending dialectic. Still others were by-products of his work as a teacher at the State Institute of Cinematography. All may be seen as notes toward that universal aesthetic theory to which his genius attracted him, and which passed through many phases as his devouring researches and astonishing capacity to learn led him on from the aesthetics of film and theatre to the history and psychology of all art, and indeed all human action.

Eisenstein's fugitive writings were first collected and published in English by his American pupil and translator, Jay Leyda, in two books, *The Film Sense* (1942) and *Film Form* (1949), the latter published after Eisenstein's death. Between these two, Eisenstein himself published in Moscow the present collection, to which its translator, X. Danko, has subsequently added three articles written later. A great many of the vast accumulation of "notes" which Eisenstein left behind have yet to be published in any language.

1969   RICHARD GRIFFITH

CONTENTS

1

ALWAYS FORWARD

LIST OF ILLUSTRATIONS

on or following page

3

FOREWORD

The cinema is undoubtedly the most international of all arts.

And not merely because films made in different countries are shown all over the world.

But first of all because with its improving techniques and growing achievements the cinema can establish a direct international contact of creative thought.

And yet in the first half century of the cinema's existence only an insignificant part of its inexhaustible resources has been used.

Please don't misunderstand me.

I am not speaking of what has been done, for much has been done that is truly excellent. As far as the content goes, first place belongs to the impetuous stream of new ideas and new ideals engendered on the screen by the new social ideas and new socialist ideals of the victorious October Revolution.

I am speaking of what *might have been done* and what cinema alone can do.

I mean those specific and unique things that can be done and created only in the realm of the cinema.

The problem of the synthesis of arts, a synthesis realizable in the cinema, has not yet found its full solution.

And in the meantime new problems are arising in increasing numbers.

No sooner have we mastered the colour technique than we have to deal with the problems of volume and space, set us by the stereoscopic cinema that is hardly out of its diapers.

Then there is the miracle of television—a living reality staring us in the face, ready to nullify the experience of the silent and sound cinema, which itself has not yet been fully assimilated.

There, montage, for instance, was a mere *sequence* (more or less perfect) of the real course of events as seen and creatively reflected through the consciousness and emotions of an artist.

Here, it will be the course of events itself, presented the moment they occur.

This will be an astonishing meeting of two extremes.

The first link in the chain of the developing forms of histrionics is the actor, the mime. Conveying to his audiences the ideas and emotions he experiences at that moment, he will hold his hand out to the exponent of the highest form of future histrionics—the TV magician—who quick as a flash will expertly use camera eyes and angles to enthral the millions-strong TV audiences with his artistic interpretation of an event taking place at that very moment.

Isn't this probable?

Isn't this possible?

Can this not be done in the era in which radar brings us echoes from the moon and aeroplanes leave the blue vault of the atmosphere at the speed of sound?

At the height of the war we dreamed that when peace came, victorious humanity would use its liberated energies to create new aesthetic values, to attain new summits of culture.

The long-awaited peace has come.

But what do we see?

The atomaniacs, drunk with the success of their monstrously destructive toy, are departing farther and farther away from the ideals of peace and unity and engendering a militarism that is even uglier than the recently overthrown idol of fascist man-haters and obscurantists.

The Soviet Union and the progressive men and women everywhere are calling for truly democratic, international cooperation.

The evil enemies of peace are doing everything to inveigle humanity into a new holocaust, into homicide and fratricide.

That is why now, as never before, the nations of the world must strive for unity and mutual understanding.

The cinema is fifty years old.* It has vast possibilities that must be used just as in the age of modern physics the atom must be used for peaceful purposes.

But how immeasurably little the world aesthetics has achieved in mastering the means and potentialities of the cinema!

It was not only because of lack of skill or enthusiasm.

It was because of striking conservatism, routine, aesthetic "escapism" in the face of new, unprecedented problems set by every new phase in the rapid development of cinematography.

We have no reason to be afraid of their onrush.

Our task is tirelessly to accumulate and sum up the experience of the ages gone by, as well as that of our own, so that, armed with this experience, we score new victories in our advance. But we should always bear in mind that *it is the profound ideological meaning of subject and content that is, and will always be, the true basis of aesthetics and that will ensure our mastery of new techniques.* The constantly improving means of expression will serve as a medium for a more perfect embodiment of lofty forms of world outlook—the lofty ideas of communism.

Constant care to preserve every grain of collective experience, however minute it may be, the burning desire to make every new thought in cinematography the property of all who create in this art, are the reason why we, Soviet film workers, have always spoken frankly of all that we are looking for, all that we find, and all that we aspire to—doing that not only through films but also through articles and treatises.

That is how my articles were born.

In selecting articles for this volume, articles that I have written

*The official birthday of the cinema is December 28, 1895, when the Brothers Lumière showed their first film at the Grand Café in the Boulevard des Capucins in Paris.—*Ed.*

over many years and on various occasions, I am moved by just one desire: to help film-makers to master all the potentialities of the cinema. This desire should motivate all who are fortunate enough to create in this singularly beautiful and unprecedentedly attractive art.

Unlike those who zealously guard their atomic "secrets" we, Soviet film-makers, cooperating closely with all our friends, will continue to share the secrets we learn over the years from our wonderful art in order to advance our common cause.

The idea of universal peace cannot be strangled by the self-love and egoism of individual countries which are prepared to sacrifice the well-being of all to satisfy their insatiable greed.

The most progressive of arts—the cinema—must be in the front ranks of this struggle, too. May it show the nations the path of solidarity and unity they should take in order to progress.

These are the feelings seething within my breast as I prepare for publication the collection of articles written at different times and in different places.

There is much that may be out of date. Much has been overcome. Much has been surpassed.

Much may be of purely historical interest, serving as landmarks on the high-road to progress during the hectic years of cinematographic quests.

Taken in their entirety, my articles, I fondly hope, will constitute a further rung in the ladder of collective experience in cinematography, which the Soviet cinema—champion of the loftiest human ideals—is ascending in spite and in defiance of all those who would drag the nations of the world back into the chaos of strife and enslavement.

Moscow-Kratovo
August, 1946

ABOUT MYSELF
AND MY FILMS

HOW I BECAME A FILM DIRECTOR

That was long ago.

Some thirty years ago.

But I distinctly remember how it started.

I mean my life in art.

Two successive impressions, like two thunderbolts, decided my fate.

The first was seeing *Turandot*, produced by F. Komissarzhevsky and staged by the Nezlobin Theatre on its tour in Riga in 1913, I believe.

From that moment the theatre became the object of my unflagging attention and boundless enthusiasm.

At that time, however, I had no intention of going on the stage and was quite content with following in my father's footsteps—with becoming a civil engineer—and had been preparing for it from my early days.

The second blow, final and irrevocable, was dealt by *Masquerade**

* *Masquerade*—a play by M. Y. Lermontov (1814-41).—*Ed.*

at the former Alexandrinsky Theatre in Petersburg, which gave shape to my longing to exchange engineering for the theatre.

Later I was profoundly grateful to fate for dealing this "blow" *after* I had passed my examinations in higher mathematics—the full university course, including the integrated differential equations—though, to tell the truth, today I have but a vague notion of what it is all about.

But I must say that my faculty to think logically and love for "mathematical" precision are undoubtedly due to my mathematical training.

No sooner had I been caught into the whirlpool of the Civil War and left the Institute of Civil Engineering than I burned all bridges behind me.

When the Civil War ended I did not return to the Institute. Instead, I plunged headlong into the theatre world.

My first job was as a designer at the First Proletcult Workers' Theatre.

After that I was a stage director.

Later I became a film director with the same company.

But it was not this that was important.

What was important was that my thirst for that mysterious thing called art was unquenchable and insatiable. No sacrifice seemed too great.

In order to be sent from the front lines to Moscow I entered the Oriental Languages Department of the General Staff Academy. To do that I had to master one thousand Japanese words and hundreds of quaint hieroglyphs.

The Academy meant more than just Moscow. It meant a possibility of learning the East, of gaining access to the fountain-head of the "magic" of art which, for me, was associated with Japan and China.

How many nights I spent memorizing words of an unknown tongue, so completely different from any of the European languages!

How different were the mnemonic methods I invented to memorize these words!

Senaka—back.

How to remember that?

Senaka—Seneca.

On the following day I check myself: covering the Japanese word with one hand I read the Russian:

Back?

Back?!

Back....

Back—Bacon!

And so on, and so forth.

Japanese is unusually difficult.

And not because there is a complete absence of sound associations with the languages we know, but because the manner of thinking resulting in word order is entirely different from the one in European languages.

Memorizing words is not the most difficult thing about the Japanese language. The most difficult thing is to master this unfamiliar method of thinking which determines the Eastern nuances of speech, structure of sentence, order of words, writing, etc.

How grateful I was to fate for having subjected me to the ordeal of learning an oriental language, opening before me that strange way of thinking and teaching me word pictography. It was precisely this "unusual" way of thinking that later helped me to master the nature of montage, and still later, when I came to recognize this "unusual," "emotional" way of thinking, different from our common "logical" way, this helped me to comprehend the most recondite in the methods of art. But of this later.

Thus my first infatuation proved to be my first true-love.

But this true-love was not all bliss; it was not only tempestuous, it was tragic.

What I always liked about Isaac Newton was his ability to ponder on falling apples and arrive at God knows what conclusions, generalizations and laws. I liked this trait so much that I provided my Alexander Nevsky with such an "apple," making this hero of the past build the strategy of the Battle on the Ice on the events of a ribald tale about a vixen and a hare, told by Ignat the armourer.

But at the dawn of my artistic career an "apple" of this kind played me a mean trick.

It was not an apple really but the chubby face of the seven-year-old son of one of the usheresses at the Proletcult Theatre, who was a frequent visitor at our rehearsals.

At one of them I looked at him and was struck by the expression on his face. It reflected not only the facial expressions or actions of some of the characters, but all that was happening on the stage at the time.

It was this simultaneousness that struck me most. I do not remember exactly if the boy's mimicry, reflecting what he saw, included inanimate objects, as did the face of a character in one of Tolstoi's works. (A servant in the count's house managed to convey through the expression of his face even the life of inanimate objects).

But gradually I began to think less of the simultaneousness of the reflection of what the boy saw—the thing that had impressed me at first—than of the nature of this reflection.

The year was 1920.

The trams were not running in Moscow.

And the long walk from the glorious boards of the theatre in Karetny Ryad,* the birth-place of so much that was remarkable on the stage, to my unheated room in Chistiye Prudy afforded me ample opportunity to ruminate on what I had seen and observed.

I was already familiar with James's famous dictum that "we weep not because we are sad; we are sad because we weep."

This formula appealed to me aesthetically—because of its paradoxic nature, in the first place, and because of the idea that a proper display of details usually associated with an emotion can arouse the emotion itself.

If such is the case, then, by reflecting facially the actions of the characters, the boy must have simultaneously and fully experienced all that the actors on the stage were experiencing—or convincingly portraying.

An adult spectator has greater command over his facial expressions, and it is perhaps for that very reason that *fictitiously*, that is, without a real cause or real action, he even more intensely lives through the entire gamut of noble and heroic feelings presented by the drama, or gives free rein in his imagination to the base and even criminal inclinations of his nature, the feelings he experiences being

* The first premises of the Moscow Art Theatre, which at this time were occupied by the Proletkult Theatre.—*Ed.*

Sergei Eisenstein against the background of a poster
announcing Ostrovsky's play *Enough Simplicity in Every
Wise Man* which he directed and designed (1923)

Author (1924)

real, though his complicity in the crimes committed on the stage is *fictitious*.

What interested me most in this argumentation was the element of "fictitiousness."

Thus art (so far in the form of theatre) enables man through co-experience *fictitiously* to perform heroic actions, *fictitiously* to experience great emotions, *fictitiously* to feel himself a hero like Franz Moor, to rid himself of base instincts with the assistance of Karl Moor, to regard himself as a sage like Faust, to feel inspired by God like Joan of Arc, to be an ardent lover like Romeo, to be a patriot like Count de Rizoor, to see his doubts dissipated by Kareno, Brand, Rosmer or Hamlet.

More. The best thing about it was that these *fictitious* actions brought the spectator real satisfaction.

Thus after seeing Verhaeren's *Les aubes* he feels he is a hero.

After seeing Calderón's *El príncipe constante* he feels he is a martyr.

After seeing Schiller's *Kabale und Liebe* he is overwhelmed by righteousness and self-pity.

"But this is horrible!" I shuddered as I was crossing Trubnaya Square (or was it Sretenskiye Gates?).

What infernal mechanics governed this sacred art whose votary I had become?

That was more than a lie!

That was more than deceit!

That was downright dangerous.

Horribly, unspeakably dangerous.

Only think: why strive for reality, if for a small sum of money you can satisfy yourself in your imagination without moving from your comfortable theatre seat?

Such were the thoughts haunting my young mind.

As I walked from Myasnitskaya Street to Pokrovskiye Gates the thoughts I pictured gradually turned into a nightmare.

Don't forget that the author was only twenty-two then.

And youth is apt to exaggerate.

Kill this nightmare!

Destroy the theatre!

I don't know whether the motives were always as chivalrous or the reasons as half-baked, but this lofty urge to kill (worthy of Raskolnikov*) obsessed other minds, too.

All around was the insistent demand to destroy art, substitute materials and documents for the chief element of art—the image, do away with its content, put constructivism in the place of organic unity, replace art itself with practical and real reconstruction of life without any fiction or fable.

The Lef** provided people of different background, mental level and aims with a common platform of active hatred for art.

But what could a mere boy who had not yet set his foot on the steps of the express train of artistic endeavour do against the public institution hallowed by centuries of history—against art—however loudly he might assail it in his breaking falsetto?

Then there came an idea:

First master art.

Then destroy it.

Penetrate into the mysteries of art.

Unveil them.

Master art.

Become a master.

And then snatch off its mask, expose it, destroy it!

That ushered in a new phase in my relations with art: the would-be murderer began playing with his intended victim.

He tried to ingratiate himself with it.

He studied it with great attention.

Just as a criminal studies the behaviour of the person he intends to victimize.

Just as a criminal spies on his victim, noting where he goes and what he does.

Noting his habits.

Noting the places he frequents.

Memorizing addresses.

Finally, accosting him.

Making his acquaintance.

* *Raskolnikov*—hero of *Crime and Punishment* by Dostoyevsky (1821-81).—*Ed.*
** *Lef*—the Left Front in Art—an organization of futurist writers and critics which existed from 1923 to 1930.—*Ed.*

A shot from *Strike* (1924)

A shot from *Strike*

Even becoming his friend.

And all the while stealthily fingering the blade of his stiletto, hoping its cold steel will remind him of his intention, will reassure him that he is not serious about the friendship.

And it was thus that we circled around each other—art and I.

It was surrounding and enthralling me by its infinite charm.

I was fingering my stiletto.

Only in my case it was not a real stiletto. It was a weapon of analysis.

In the transition period, pending the "final act," the dethroned goddess, I decided on closer acquaintance with her, would be useful for the common cause.

She was not worthy of wearing the crown.

Why shouldn't she scrub floors for a while?

Influencing minds through art was, after all, something.

And if the young proletarian state was to fulfil the urgent tasks confronting it, it had to exert a lot of influence on hearts and minds.

Once I studied mathematics.

It would seem I had wasted my time (although later, when I least expected it, it proved useful).

Once I slaved learning Japanese hieroglyphs.

Again it seemed a waste of time.

(At that time I did not perceive their usefulness. I realized, even then, that there existed different systems of thinking, but I never suspected this would be of any use to me.)

Well, now there was the method of art to be learned.

And here there was at least the advantage of making good use of the period of learning itself.

So once again I plunged into books and notebooks. Once again there were laboratory analyses, experiments, the Periodic Law of Mendeleyev, the laws of Gay-Lussac and Boyle and Mariotte—in art.

And then an unforeseen thing occurred!

The young engineer set down to business.

And found himself completely at a loss.

Every other line of the theoretical analysis of his new and enchanting acquaintance—the theory of art—was enshrouded with seven veils of mystery.

And ocean of gauze!

As if it were a ball dress from Paquin.

But then it is well known that a sword cannot chop up a feather pillow. And no sword, however heavy and sharp, would enable one to cut through this ocean of gauze.

A feather pillow can be cut up only with a sharp scimitar wielded by an experienced warrior—a Saladdin or a Suleiman.

A frontal attack would be of no avail.

The curvature of the scimitar is symbolic of the roundabout way to take to fathom the mysteries behind the seven veils.

But that was all right, we were young and had plenty of time. The whole of the future.

The daring creative ideas of the twenties were bubbling all around.

They manifested themselves in exuberant young sprouts of crazy imagination, mad inventions, infinite boldness.

And all this was prompted by a burning desire to find some new, unknown means of expressing new experiences.

But, in defiance of the banished term "creation" (substituted by "work"), in spite of "construction" whose bony tentacles were spread out to strangle the image, the exciting epoch gave birth to one creative (yes, *creative*) achievement after another.

For the time being, art and its would-be murderer created side by side in the unique and unforgettable atmosphere of the early twenties.

Still the murderer was not forgetting his stiletto.

As I have said, the stiletto was a weapon of analysis.

Don't forget it was a young engineer who was bent on finding a scientific approach to the secrets and mysteries of art.

The disciplines he had studied had taught him one thing: in every scientific investigation there must be a unit of measurement.

So he set out in search of the unit of impression produced by art! Science knows "ions," "electrons," "neutrons."

Let there be "attractions" in art.

Each line of the script blossomed out into a scene because the emotional impact was produced not by these cursory lines in the script, but by a whole gamut of feelings and associations giving rise to live images as soon as mention was made of an event long familiar.

So, without endangering veracity, we could give free rein to imagination, enriching our work with action not provided for by the script (the Odessa steps) and with details that sprang up on the spur of the moment (mist in the mourning scene).

But there is one more thing for which I must thank Nina Agadzhanova—bringing me through the revolutionary past to the revolutionary present.

The intellectuals who embraced the Revolution after 1917 invariably passed through the stage of opposing *I* to *they*, before they finally saw the two blended in the Soviet revolutionary *we*.

The diminutive blue-eyed Nuneh (the Armenian for Nina) Agadzhanova, so modest, shy and sweet, guided me well through that transition phase.

And I am deeply grateful to her for that.

1

To make a motion picture about a battleship, you must have a battleship.

To re-create the history of a 1905 battleship, it had to be of the type in use at the time.

War craft had undergone radical changes in appearance in the two decades since 1905 (this was in the summer of 1925).

At that time a ship of the old type could no longer be found in the Baltic Fleet or in the Black Sea Fleet.

The cruiser we saw rocking merrily in the Sevastopol roadsteads was not the thing we needed. She did not have the characteristic round stern and quarter-deck—the scene of the famous dramatic episode we were to reproduce.

The *Potemkin* herself had long been dismantled and it would have been in vain to try tracing the steel plates of armour that used to protect her boards.

But then our "scouts" reported that although the *Prince Potemkin of Taurida* was no more, there existed her sister-ship, the once famed and mighty *Twelve Apostles*.

Chained to the rocky shore, her anchors deep in the sandy sea bottom, the heroic ship of bygone days was hidden in a remote bend of the bay.

The tortuous arms of the bay going deep under the mountains teemed with hundreds and thousands of mines. The oblong greyish-rusty hulk of the *Twelve Apostles* like a watchful Cerberus was guarding the entrance to the caves.

The broad back of this sleeping whale, however, was bare of turrets, masts, flagstaffs and bridge.

Time and tide had washed them away.

Now and then her many-tiered holds would resound to the rumble of cars transporting the heavy and lethal contents of her metal vaults: mines, mines, mines.

The *Twelve Apostles* had been converted into a mine dump. That is why she was so securely moored. Mines objected to jolts and shocks: they liked calmness and tranquillity.

It seemed the *Twelve Apostles* was doomed for ever to lie immovably in the quiet waters of the Bay of Sevastopol.

But the iron whale was fated to awaken once again.

It was once more to move.

Once again its prow, seemingly so securely fastened to the mountains, was to be turned seaward.

The battleship lay off and parallel to the rocky shore.

But the drama on the quarter-deck had taken place in the open sea.

It was impossible to shoot any scenes from one of the boards or the stem without getting formidable steep black crags in the background.

But the keen-eyed Lyosha Kryukov, one of my assistants, who had unearthed the old-timer in the bay, found a way out of the difficulty.

Moved 90°, the ponderous hulk of the ship was placed perpendicular to the shore, her façade shot from the stem appearing opposite a cleave between two great crags, her silhouette outlined against the background of a clear sky.

And the effect obtained was that of a ship at sea.*

Startled seagulls who had thought the ship was a crag circled over her, enhancing the illusion of the open sea.

The iron whale was moving amidst a tense silence.

The Black Sea command issued special orders which once more made the iron giant face the sea.

And the battleship seemed to be drawing in the salt air of the sea, so invigorating after the reeking stagnation in the cove.

The mines piled up in her holds probably did not notice anything as her heavy bulk started turning smoothly.

But they could not help awakening to the sound of the axe: on the ship's deck the upper quarters of the *Potemkin* were being rebuilt of plywood in accordance with the old blueprints preserved at the Admiralty.

This was symbolic: on the basis of real history the film re-created the past by means of art.

Sharp turns either to right or left were strictly to be avoided.

The ship must not be moved an inch.

For that would destroy the illusion of the open sea.

And the ancient crags would peep gleefully into the camera eye.

These strict demands of space hampered our movements.

The time demands were no less strict: the film had to be ready by the anniversary date and this proved a restraint on our imagination.

Chains and anchors held tight the old hulk of a battleship that was rearing to go out to sea.

The chains and anchors of space and time restricted our eager imagination.

And perhaps this accounted for the austerity of the film.

Mines, mines, mines.

It is only natural that they should pop up from under my pen as I write this. Mines dominated all our work.

No smoking.

No running.

As soon as your business is over on the deck—clear off.

---

* True, there is a side view of the battleship in the film, but this was shot ... in the "Moorish" swimming-pool of the Sandunov Public Baths in Moscow, with a miniature model of the war vessel proudly riding the tepid "waves" of the pool. —*Author's Note.*

But more terrible than the mines was the guard, Comrade Glazastikov.

Yes, Glazastikov,* this is no pun. And he (alas!) proved worthy of his name, which aptly described this ever alert Argus guarding the tiers of mines under our feet against fire, against shocks, against detonation.

It would have taken months to unload the mines and all we had was a mere fortnight to finish the film for the anniversary date.

Hard work that—filming an uprising in such conditions!

But "Russians are not daunted by obstacles" and the uprising *was* filmed.

So it was not in vain that the mines in the hold of the old battleship were disturbed or that the uproar of the historical events recreated on her deck made them quiver. The ship on the screen seemed imbued with their explosive power.

The screen image of the old rebel gave a headache to censors, police forces and police pickets in many a European country.

And true to its reputation of a rebel, it caused quite a revolution in film aesthetics.

2

Potemkin had made its round of Russian cinemas and was due to be released in the Ukraine.

Its appearance there caused quite an uproar.

And the charge was ... plagiarism.

Its author was a man who claimed he had taken part in the *Potemkin* mutiny.

What he wanted remains a mystery to this day, for he had never written anything about the mutiny.

But since he had participated in it, he thought he was entitled to a share of the fees due to script-writer Agadzhanova and myself.

His claim was vague, noisy and not very intelligible.

But the assertion that he "was under the tarpaulin during the shooting on the quarter-deck" was impressive and eventually the case was brought to court.

* Glazastikov—from Russian *glaz*—an eye. Hence, big-eyed.—*Tr.*

Eisenstein directing the camera crew of *Potemkin* (courtesy
The Museum of Modern Art/Film Stills Archive)

Eisenstein and the camera crew of *Potemkin* (courtesy The Museum of Modern Art/Film Stills Archive)

This seemed an incontestable proof, and the lawyers were about to demand damages in favour of the plaintiff when the whole noisy affair was blown sky-high.

The thing that caused it was a circumstance which the producers themselves had forgotten at the time.

The man asserted he "was under the tarpaulin."

But the fact was ... there was no one under the tarpaulin.

No one could have been there. ...

For the simple reason that no one on the *Potemkin* had been *covered* with a tarpaulin.

The scene where the sailors are covered with a tarpaulin was the director's invention.

I remember perfectly well a former naval officer, who was my adviser and who played Matyushenko, grabbing his head and remonstrating against the idea of covering the sailors with a tarpaulin before the execution.

"We shall be ridiculed!" he stormed. "This was never done!"

And then he explained that a tarpaulin used to be brought to the deck before sailors were to be shot but that the condemned were made to stand on it to keep the deck clean of blood.

"And here you are covering the sailors with the tarpaulin. We'll make a laughing-stock of ourselves!"

I remember retorting:

"If we do it will serve us right for bungling our job."

And I ordered the scene to be shot the way you see it in the film.

It was subsequently this very detail (the isolation of the condemned from life) that proved to be one of the most effective.

This gigantic "bandage" covering the eyes of the condemned, this shroud placed over living men was so emotionally convincing that the technical inaccuracy (besides, only specialists knew it for such) passed completely unnoticed.

This fully confirmed Goethe's statement that "for the sake of truthfulness one can afford to defy the truth."

That was the undoing of our formidable opponent who claimed to have been under the tarpaulin when the sailors were shot on the quarter-deck. And although there seemed to be some "truthfulness" in his statement, he was defeated.

The scene was left in the film as it was.

It became part and parcel of the historical event.

And, most important of all, it was never ridiculed.

Film fans are interested not only in the characters but in the actors, too. I will say a few words about some of them.

One of the leading characters was a surgeon and we sought long and fruitlessly for a suitable type, finally chosing an actor with whom we were not fully satisfied.

I was taking my unit, including the "surgeon," in a launch to the cruiser *Comintern* to film the episode with the maggoty meat.

I sat sulking as far from the "surgeon" as possible, not looking his way.

I knew the Sevastopol port inside out.

I was sick of the actors' faces, too.

My eye roamed over the faces of the men who would hold the mirrors and reflectors during the shooting.

One of them was a small, puny man.

He was a stove-heater in the cold, draughty hotel where we spent our free time.

"What's the idea of hiring such weaklings to hold the heavy mirrors?" I wondered. "He might drop the mirror into the water. Or break it. And that's a bad omen."

Here my mind switched from assessing his physical qualifications as a workman to his expressive properties. He had small moustaches and a goatee. . . . Cunning eyes. . . . I imagined him wearing *pince-nez* with a thin chain. . . . I saw him in a naval surgeon's cap instead of in the greasy thing he was wearing.

By the time we had reached the cruiser to shoot the scene my idea became a reality: the *Potemkin* surgeon, but a few moments before that an honest workman, was superciliously eyeing the maggoty meat through his *pince-nez*.

Rumour still persists that I played the priest.

That's not true.

The priest was portrayed by an old gardener from the orchards on the outskirts of Sevastopol. The beard was his own, slightly parted. The hair was not. It was a perfectly white wig.

The rumour spread after the publication of a photograph showing the make-up artist pasting a beard on my chin as I sit in the priest's wig and cassock. I was doubling for the old gardener in the scene where he had to fall down the stairs with his back turned to the camera. The idea of performing the stunt was too tempting.

The third participant has remained anonymous, too. More than that, he does not appear in the picture.

And thank God for that, for he was more of an enemy of the film than a participant in it.

The man was the park watchman of Alupka Palace in the Crimea.

His worn boots and shabby pants narrowly missed appearing on the screen, as he stubbornly sat on the head of one of the lions demanding that we get a special permit to photograph it.

But since there are six lions gracing the stairs we rushed with our cameras from one to another, leading this strict but foolish "limb of the law" such a dance that he finally let us be, and we managed to shoot close-ups of three marble beasts.

The "leaping lions," too, were an inspiration: it descended upon us at Alupka where we were spending a "wasted" day.

The famous "fog sequence...."

A heavy mist hung over the port. The mirror-like bay seemed to be enveloped in cotton wool. If *Swan Lake* were presented here, among portal cranes and winches, and not at the Opera House in Odessa, one might think that these were the snow-white robes of the maidens who had become white swans and flown away.

Reality, however, is more prosaic. A mist means a "wasted day," a Black Friday in the shooting schedule.

Sometimes there were actually seven such Fridays in a week!

That particular day, too, was a Black Friday, although everything around was as white as white could be. The only black objects were the cranes sticking out from among the orange blossoms of mist. Also, the black hulls of boats, barges and merchantmen, resembling hippopotamuses caught in gauze.

Here and there, the fluffed lint of fog was pierced by a few threads of sun-rays imparting to it a warm, golden-rosy tint.

But the sun pulled over its face a veil of clouds, as if envious of its own reflection in the sea, enveloped in the swan down of mist.

All that was very good, but work was out of the question.

We hired a boat for 3.50 rubles.

Tisse, Alexandrov and I went boating in the misty harbour which looked as if it were covered with apple-blossoms.

Three men in a boat....

Our camera, like a faithful dog, was with us. And like ourselves, it was hoping for a rest. But the three men were enthusiasts and it had to work, photographing the mist.

The mist stuck to the lens of the camera like wool sticks between teeth.

The gears of the camera seemed to whisper, "Things like that should not be filmed." This opinion was shared by the occupants of a passing boat:

"A rum lot!"

This was uttered by cameraman L. who was in Odessa making a film. His Quixotian figure sprawled leisurely in the boat. Appearing and disappearing in the mist, he ironically wished us luck.

And we *were* lucky.

The chance encounter with mists which suddenly acquired an emotional content, the choice of details, the individual shots were combined at once into plastic mournful chords, to produce later, in the process of montage, a funeral symphony in memory of Vakulinchuk.

This scene was the least expensive in the picture: it cost only 3.50 rubles which we paid for the hire of the boat.

3

The Odessa steps were one more inspiration of the moment.

It is my opinion that at the moment of shooting the scenery, sets and props are often wiser than the director.

One must be really gifted and greatly skilled to be able to hear and understand what the scenes suggest, to be able to listen as one edits the film to the whispering of the shots which, on the screen, live a life of their own, frequently extending beyond the limits of the imagination that has conceived them.

But to be able to do this, the director must have an exceptionally clear idea of every scene or phase of the film. At the same time he must be versatile in choosing the means for expressing his ideas.

He must be sufficiently pedantic to know how to achieve the desired effect and at the same time liberal enough to accept unforeseen objects and means that are capable of producing this effect.

Scene from the mist sequence in *Potemkin*

A shot from the Odessa steps sequence in *Potemkin*

The working script contains the exact degree of tension reached when the shooting on the Odessa steps is cut short by gunfire from *Potemkin*. The draft copy lists the means for obtaining this tension.

Chance suggested a more forceful and impressive solution in the same key, and the fortuitous became an integral component part of the film.

The working script had dozens of pages elaborating the mourning over the body of Vakulinchuk, expressed in the slow movements of harbour facilities.

We chanced to see them floating dreamily in the misty harbour, and their emotional impact fitted in perfectly with the idea of mourning, and so the chance mist became the core of our conception.

The sequence of episodes showing Cossack brutalities in mounting crescendo (in the street, in the print-shop yard, on the outskirts and in front of the bakery), in a rising scale whose steps constitute the tragedy's natural links, was arrived at in a similar way.

Neither the original script nor the montage drafts provided for the shooting scene on the Odessa steps. The idea flashed in my mind when I saw the steps.

The assertion that it was born as I stood at the foot of the Duke's* monument and watched the cherry-stones I was spitting out hop down the steps is a myth. A colourful one, but a myth just the same. The flight of the steps suggested the scene and gave an impulse to a new flight of imagination. It would be right to say that the stampede of the panic-stricken crowd down the steps is nothing but an embodiment of the sensations I experienced at seeing them for the first time.

Another source might have been the dim recollection of an illustration I had seen in a 1905 magazine, showing a horseman on the smoke-enveloped steps, slashing right and left with his sword.

Be that as it may, the scene on the Odessa steps became one of the most important in the film.

The stove-heater, the mist, the steps—they all repeated the history of the film, itself created from the rib of the voluminous scenario of *The Year 1905*, embracing an enormous number of events.

I must confess that the Sun does not call on me, as it did on the

---

* The monument to the Duke de Richelieu.—*Ed.*

late Mayakovsky, for a cup of tea.* Still, now and then, quite unexpectedly, it does me a favour. It was considerate enough to shine non-stop for 40 days in 1938 while we were shooting the Battle on the Ice for *Alexander Nevsky* at the Mosfilm lot.

And it was the Sun that made us pack up and leave Leningrad in 1925, when we launched somewhat belatedly to shoot *1905*. It made us chase for its last beams in Odessa and Sevastopol and compelled us to choose from the scenario the only episode that could be filmed in the south.

And that one particular episode became the emotional embodiment of the whole epic of 1905.

A part took the place of the whole.

And absorbed the emotions of the whole.

How was this achieved?

A feature of this film was that close-ups, which usually served as explanatory details, became the parts capable of evoking the whole in the perception and feelings of the spectator.

This was how the surgeon's *pince-nez* was utilized: the dangling eye-glasses were made to symbolize their owner, helplessly struggling among the seaweeds after the sailors had thrown him overboard.

In one of my articles I compared this method of treating close-ups with a figure of speech known as synecdoche. I think both depend on the ability of our consciousness to reconstruct (mentally and emotionally) the whole from a part.

But when can this phenomenon be relied on as an artistic method? When can a particular episode take the place of the whole logically and completely?

Only in cases where the detail, the part, the particular episode is typical. In other words, when it reflects the whole like a piece of broken mirror.

The image of this surgeon with his goatee and physical and mental short-sightedness is ideally expressed by the characteristic form of the *pince-nez* worn in 1905, usually fastened to one ear by a chain.

Similarly, this particular episode of the *Potemkin* uprising was made up of events highly characteristic of the 1905 Revolution ("the dress rehearsal for the October Revolution").

---

* Eisenstein means Mayakovsky's poem entitled *The Wonderful Experiences of Vladimir Mayakovsky in the Country.—Ed.*

Maggoty meat became a symbol of the inhuman conditions in which the whole mass of the exploited classes, and not only the army and navy, lived.

The quarter-deck scene is equally characteristic of the cruelty with which tsarism crushed every attempt at protest, wherever and whenever it was made.

Another event, not less characteristic of 1905, was the reaction of those who were ordered to fire on the rebels.

The refusal to shoot at the crowd, the masses, the people, at their own brothers, was extremely typical of the time, and many a military unit sent by the reactionaries to crush uprisings prided itself on that.

The mourning over the body of Vakulinchuk was one of the countless instances when the funerals of revolutionary heroes became impassioned demonstrations and led to new uprisings followed by fierce reprisals. The Vakulinchuk scene reproduced the emotions and destinies of those who carried Bauman's dead body through the streets of Moscow.

The scene on the Odessa steps is a synthesis of the slaughter in Baku and the January 9 Massacre, when "credulous crowds" were rejoicing at the invigorating breath of freedom of 1905 and when the reactionaries destroyed these hopes as ruthlessly as the Black Hundred pogromists who set fire to a theatre in Tomsk where a meeting was in progress.

And the finale of the film with the battleship sailing majestically past the Admiral's squadron, cutting short the events of the film at a major note, is symbolic of the 1905 Revolution as a whole.

We know what happened to *Potemkin* later: she was interned at Constanza and then handed back to the tsarist government. Some of the sailors escaped. But Matyushenko was executed by the tsar's hangmen.

But we were quite justified in ending the film with the historical battleship victorious. Because the 1905 Revolution itself, though drowned in blood, has gone down in history as an objectively victorious episode, the harbinger of the triumph of the October Revolution.

This triumphantly presented episode of defeat stresses all the more forcibly the importance of the great events of 1905, of which the *Potemkin* was no more than an individual episode, but one reflecting the greatness of the whole.

To return to anonymous actors.... With the exception of Antonov who played Vakulinchuk, Grigory Alexandrov—Gilyarovsky, the late director Barsky, who played Golikov, and the boatswain Levchenko whose whistle was very helpful to us, the players have remained unknown.

What has become of the hundreds of these anonymous people who brought to the film their unflagging enthusiasm, who ran up and down the steps under the scorching sun, who marched in the endless procession of mourners?

I would like most of all to meet the nameless child crying in his pram as it went rolling down the steps.

He must be twenty now. Where is he? What is he doing? Was he among the defenders of Odessa? Does he lie buried in the common grave at the estuary off Odessa? Or is he busy rebuilding his native city?

I remember the names of some of the participants in the mass scenes.

I have a good reason for this.

This is a "Napoleonic trick" widely used by directors.

Napoleon was in the habit of learning about the personal affairs of his soldiers from their friends and then astonishing them by asking: "How's your sweetheart Loison?" "How are your parents—the kind Rosalie and the industrious Tibault—getting on? What about your little house on the outskirts of St. Tropez?" "How is Aunt Justine's gout?"

The crowd is rushing down the stairs, more than a thousand pairs of feet. The first time they do it fairly well. The second there is less energy. The third time they move positively slowly.

All of a sudden from an elevation, drowning out the stamping of boots and sandals, comes the director's voice booming through the megaphone:

"Put more pep into it, Comrade Prokopenko!"

The crowd is dumbfounded: "Can he see every one of us from that damned platform? Does he know our names?"

The crowd feels a new upsurge of energy and rushes onwards,

everyone quite certain that the director's watchful eyes is on him.

And all he has done really is to shout the name of a man he knows.

*   *   *

In addition to the thousands of anonymous players there were some anonyms in a class by themselves.

These anonyms were the cause of anxiety on an international scale —they were the subject of an interpellation in the Reichstag.

The anonyms were the ships of the Admiral's squadron menacingly crowding the *Potemkin* in the final scene.

They were many and formidable.

Their number was many times over that of the fleet the young Soviet country had in 1925.

That was the cause of our German neighbour's alarm.

So the intelligence on Soviet military strength collected by spies was incorrect and incomplete?!

That was the reason for the question on the exact strength of the Soviet fleet.

Fear breeds terror. And the eyes of the terror-stricken observers failed to see that the shots showing the formidable squadrons were taken from an old newsreel of the manoeuvres of some foreign navy.

Years have passed. Our fleet has become an awe-inspiring reality. And the memory of the rebellious battleship is fresh in the hearts of its numerous steel offspring.

Here I must pay tribute to the chief anonym, not an actor, but the anonymous author:

to our great Russian people;

to its heroic revolutionary past;

to its great creative inspiration, the inexhaustible fountain-head of inspiration for our artists.

Let all who create in our country express here their warmest thanks to the millions—the source of inspiration and true authors of all our endeavours.

1945

ALEXANDER NEVSKY

Bones. Skulls. Scorched fields. Charred ruins of human dwellings. People enslaved and driven far from home. Plundered towns. Human dignity trampled underfoot. Such is the awesome picture rising before us as we think of the early thirteenth-century Russia. Having laid waste the flourishing Georgia with her ancient culture in the Caucasus, the Mongol-Tatar hordes of Genghis Khan skirted the Caspian from the south and struck at Russia bringing with them horror, death and bewilderment—whence this terrible force?

The utter defeat suffered at Kalka in 1223 by the Russian troops sent to oppose this force was merely a prelude to the bloody epic of Baty's invasion which shook the whole of Europe.

Russian principalities and cities were ready to repulse the formidable foe. But they were not mature enough to realize that internecine wars and feuds were not the way to found a powerful state capable of opposing any invader. Divided, they displayed great courage, but were destroyed one by one in unequal strife. The Tatars were advancing at an appalling pace and threatened to overrun Europe. Appeals for collective action found no response in panic-stricken Europe.

In the meantime, the Kiev state and the other component parts of the then divided Russia, languished under the yoke of the avid conqueror who plundered what had remained of the subjugated and oppressed principalities. Such was the picture of the long-suffering Russia in the thirteenth century. Unless one had a clear idea of this state of things, one could never understand the magnificent heroism displayed by the Russian people who, though enslaved by the barbarous Eastern nomads, rallied round the glorious Alexander Nevsky to rout the Teutons when the latter stretched their tentacles to grab a slice of Russian soil.

Whence came the Teutonic Knights? The Teutonic House was founded early in the twelfth century, first in Jerusalem and subsequently in Ptolemaïs which was then besieged by the Crusaders. It became the scourge of mankind and, like leprosy, spread over Eastern and Western Europe.

At first the Teutonic House was a simple field hospital, but the Teutons were very active in it. On February 6, 1191, the Order of Teutonic Knights was founded with Rome's blessing. On July 12 of that year, the Crusaders took Ptolemaïs and the new Order got a considerable share of the spoils—it received lands and other property and settled down on conquered territory. It thus acquired a centre from which to direct its activities and henceforth the Order united not only the Teutonic elements of Palestine but of the whole of Europe. Its composition was of a pronouncedly national and caste character: only Germans of noble birth were eligible for membership.

At first, the knights confined their activities to selling their military skill. But soon they launched on a steady and systematic drive eastward. The victims of this expansion were successively the Prussians, the Livonians, the Esthes, the Zhmud. Rivalling the Tatars in cruel and merciless treatment of the conquered people, the Teutons (by that time united with other monastic and no less predatory Orders) surpassed them in at least one way. Whereas the former were content with raiding, plundering and laying waste the conquered territories and usually went back to the Asiatic steppes or to the lands of the horde after laying a heavy, often unbearable, contribution on the vanquished, the Teutonic and Livonian knights systematically colonized the conquered countries, enslaving the people and destroying all national characteristics, religion and social order.

Superior in war equipment and organization, the "pious brothers" were not averse to using any and every means, notably recruiting traitors.

Along with the names of the heroic defenders of Russia, the annals have preserved the names of such despicable traitors as Prince Vladimir of Pskov, his equally treacherous son Yaroslav, and Tverdila Ivankovich, the notorious Pskov mayor who betrayed Pskov to the Germans out of purely mercenary motives.

Resistance (and later, organized counter-offensive) to Western invaders came from Novgorod. The glorious name of Novgorod is for ever associated with the renaissance of national independence, which was the goal of all far-sighted and patriotic princes. Foremost among them was Prince Alexander of Novgorod, called Nevsky, whose strength lay not only in his talent but in his ties with the peasant militia whom he led in many a victorious campaign. These ties with the people provided him with a compass which enabled him unerringly to steer his course in the complex international situation of the time and choose the only historically correct road. By cajoling the Tatars and doing his best to be on friendly terms with them, Alexander secured for himself freedom of action in the West whence loomed the greatest danger to the Russian people and to the first shoots of national consciousness engendered by aggression from East and West. Alexander decided to deliver his first blow at the Germans.

The Battle on the Ice, fought on Lake Chudskoye on April 5, 1242, crowned the successful campaign he waged together with his peasant militia. It was the climax of the brilliantly planned military campaign against the invader who tried to check the advance of Alexander's vanguard at Izborsk and to encircle his main force. Alexander divined the German plan and, surprising the enemy by a vanguard manoeuvre, stopped him on the western bank of the lake, close to the mouth of the Embach. Numerically overwhelmed, the vanguard, under the command of the valiant Domash Tverdislavich and Kerbet, was defeated. Undaunted, Alexander retreated to the frozen Lake Chudskoye and, without crossing to the eastern (Russian) bank, resolved to engage the Germans at the gulf joining lakes Chudskoye and Pskovskoye. The Teutons attacked in the terrible, invincible wedge formation.

Let us picture to ourselves this formation, formerly considered invincible. Imagine the stem of a battleship or a powerful tank magnified to the size of one hundred iron-clad horsemen advancing in serried ranks. Imagine this gigantic iron triangle advancing at full gallop and gathering momentum. Imagine, finally, the "thin edge" of this giant iron wedge cutting into the very midst of the enemy soldiers, stupefied by the terrible mass of steel bearing down upon them: instead of the knights' faces they see steel visors with cross-shaped openings. No sooner does the wedge split the enemy front than it breaks up into so many "spears," each "spear" being an iron-clad knight (the prototype of a light tank), cutting his way through the living mass of the enemy soldiers and felling them right and left. The comparison with a light tank becomes all the more convincing when we recall that a "spear" was not one knight but a whole group of men (sometimes thirteen) consisting of armour-bearers, pages, knaves, horsemen, all acting at one with the knight.

With the state of military art as it was in those days it was as impossible to withstand the attack of a wedge as trying to stop a tank with bare hands is today.

Alexander Nevsky employed against the Germans the same brilliant manoeuvre which had covered Hannibal with glory in the Battle of Cannae. He knew that the centre could not hold back the attack of the wedge and he did not attempt the impossible. He concentrated his main forces on the flanks, so that the weak centre gave way before the wedge and drew it in. To the envy of the generals of the future, Alexander succeeded in completely surrounding the enemy with the troops on the flanks. Moreover, a regiment lying in ambush cut into the enemy rear, and the insidious foe, caught in a circle, was routed. Earlier history had never known such a battle. The Germans had never sustained such defeat. The pages of the chronicles are filled with the din and cries of the battle: "The snapping of spears, the clash of swords—one would think the frozen lake had come alive. . . . The ice could not be seen for the blood covering it. . . and the Russian warriors slashed at them, pursuing them as if in the air, and they had nowhere to flee. . . . They were massacred on the ice all the seven versts to the Subolich bank."

One may ask, why was the battle fought on ice? There are many explanations for this: the smooth surface of the frozen lake made it possible to face the enemy (the Russians had always fought on plains); it was easy to form the troops in the desired order; the slippery surface impeded the pace of the horsemen; and, finally, it was thought the ice would break under the knights and their heavy armour. And this actually happened when the pursued knights crowded in front of the steep western bank which was slowing down their flight. The April ice, which was thinner near the bank, gave way and the remaining fugitives met their end in the cold waters.

The defeat of the Teutonic Knights on Lake Chudskoye was an unexpected, breath-taking miracle.* The chroniclers sought an explanation of this miracle in supernatural phenomena; they speak of heavenly hosts taking part in the battle. But the victory was, of course, due not to these doubtful predecessors of modern aviation: the only miraculous thing in the Battle on the Ice was the genius of the Russian people, who, for the first time in history, became conscious of their strength as a nation, of their unity. And this awakening conscious-

* A play on words. Miracle in Russian is *chudo,* from which the lake derives its name.—*Tr.*

ness proved a source of their invincible strength. Alexander, a gifted strategist and general, came from their midst and led them to defend their native country and destroy the wily foe. This is the fate in store for all who may dare attack our country. For if the spiritual strength of the people was such as to defeat an enemy at a time when the country was languishing under the Tatar yoke, there is no force capable of shattering it when it is free from all shackles, from all oppression, when it has become a socialist state.*

* * *

A few broken broadswords, a helmet and a couple of chain mails preserved in museums are all the relics of those far-off times.

All we knew when we started work on the film was that the thirteenth century was "hoary antiquity" and that its hero was a saint.

This epithet seemed misleading at first, and there was a danger of overlooking in the hero a sober, real and strong statesman, very much of this world and bone of the bone of his people. His physical appearance, too, was highly exaggerated: "The nobility of his bearing, the majesty of his person were such as to eclipse not only all his kinsmen, but the kings of all the other countries in the world, as does the Sun all other heavenly bodies...." and "He is taller than any man on earth, his voice is like a clarion call, in visage he is like Joseph the Beautiful whom the Egyptian king made the second king in Egypt, in strength he was second only to Samson, and God hath given him the wisdom of Solomon and the courage of the Roman King Vespasian who conquered the whole of Judea."

"His voice is like a clarion call"—should such voice thunder from the screen? Should we overwhelm our spectators with the superlatives of the chronicler?

And yet in the heaps of disconnected data, the queer-sounding terminology of the chronicles, the fantastic drawings in old miniatures and the lives of the saints there pulsates the constant, insistent, unswerving rhythm of the main theme.

It permeates the scanty works on the material culture of that epoch.

---

* This was written two years before the treacherous German invasion of our country.—*Author's Note.*

36

It pulsates in the rust-eaten relics preserved from those days. It breathes in the turrets and walls of ancient fortresses and towns.

Touching the old buildings of Novgorod, I quoted Surikov: "I believed stones, not books." The stones, it seemed, embodied the theme; it rang in each stone, one and the same theme from beginning to end, the theme of national pride, strength, love of Motherland, the theme of patriotism of the Russian people.

The "formalist" temptations left me. The Gordian knots untied themselves.

I was seized with the profound feeling that I was making a film that was, first and foremost, a *contemporary* one: the striking thing was the similarity between the events described in the chronicles and epics and the events of our own days.

In spirit, if not in letter, the events of the thirteenth century are emotionally close to ours. And, for that matter, in letter, too. I shall never forget the day when, having just read in a paper about the savage destruction of Guernica by the fascists, I turned to historical records and found a description of the capture of Gersik by the Crusaders.* This determined still more clearly the creative and stylistic treatment of the material.

Now and again I was assailed with doubts: how would it look if the leader of the Teutonic-Livonian knights conversed with Tverdila, the treacherous Pskov mayor, in fluent Russian, without an interpreter translating the incomprehensible thirteenth-century German into the scarcely more comprehensible Russian of that time? Perhaps the thirteenth-century interventionists were as good linguists as the aggressors who stretched their filthy talons towards our country from East and West in the twentieth century. But then Russian would be spoken in the scenes where the "brother knights" divide among

---

* "... Then came the turn of Gersik. The ruling prince of that province was Vsevolod, a sworn enemy of the Romans. Bishop Albert had elaborated an insidious plan for taking Gersik by surprise. The plan succeeded. The prince just managed to escape in a boat; his wife and the entire household fell into the hands of the enemy. The town was sacked. The atrocities lasted the whole day. On the next day, the Germans set fire to the town and departed, taking booty and captives. Vsevolod was on the opposite bank of the Dvina. Seeing the town in flames, he exclaimed: 'O Gersik, Gersik, my beloved town, the home of my fathers! Woe that I should have lived to see thee on fire and my people perishing!' " (From a biography of Alexander Nevsky published in 1893) —*Author's Note.*

themselves lands which remain to be conquered or where the Bishop says (and he spoke Latin, of course) that the sway of Rome must spread to everything.

But the doubts dissipated even faster than they arose when I asked myself the following questions:

What is more important for the spectator—to hear the strange rhythm and sound of a foreign tongue and have to read captions, or to be introduced without loss of time and energy to such tragic events as betrayal, maltreatment of the conquered people and the scope of the knights' aggressive aspirations?

What is more important: to make a research into languages of six hundred years ago or to hear Alexander Nevsky describe in good modern Russian his plan for distributing forces before the Battle on the Ice, a plan providing for the defeat of the enemy on his own territory?

There can be no doubt that the second proposition was the more important. In both instances. And in all other instances where certain words had to drive home to the spectator the essence and meaning of the events presented on the screen. No other words were necessary. Hence the relative laconism of the film's text, although there is no lack of dialogue in it.

How did the people walk in the thirteenth century? How did they speak? How did they eat? How did they stand? Should we screen beautiful stylizations of the type of the high reliefs on the bronze gate of St. Sophia's Cathedral, or the somewhat less ancient illustrations in the Königsberg Chronicle? How should we show the costume suggesting the icons of the Novgorod school? How should we establish living contact with those people, so far and yet so near to us?

I stood on the walls of their town, looked from the battlements at the landscape that had met their eyes and tried to imagine what they saw. I tried to capture the rhythm of their movements by touching the few articles that have come down to us: a pair of mildewed boots with pointed toes fished out of the marshy Volkhov, a vessel, an ornament worn on the breast. I tried to puzzle out the way they walked by treading on the wooden pavements of Novgorod or on the layer of ground animal bones with which its Town Square was paved. But all that was in vain, it was not the thing. All this led to was either a waxworks exhibition or unskilled stylization.

And here, too, everything suddenly became clear.

We admired the inimitable perfection of the Church of Spas-Nereditsa.* It would be hard to find any building equalling this twelfth-century monument for purity of line and harmony of proportions. Its stones saw Alexander and Alexander saw them. We walked around it as we had walked over Alexander Hill in Pereyaslavl, an artificial mound on the shore of Lake Pleshcheyevo. The building was beautiful but the common language we were looking for was still that of aesthetics, of proportions and pure lines. We lacked direct communion, a psychological penetration into the monument; we lacked a living language. Suddenly we saw a tablet placed by the considerate staff of the museum; it carried a few lines which seemed to have no bearing on the matter at hand: "Construction began in ... completed in...." At first glance there seemed to be nothing special in that, but when you subtracted the first date from the second you saw that its construction took only a few months in the twelfth century.

Reading the tablet engendered a new outlook on the stone pillars, arches and vaults: you saw them grow dynamically, you sensed the dynamics of human labour; you did not observe the acts from without, you sensed the acts, deeds, creative efforts from within. They were close to us, they were tangible, and over the span of centuries they were connected with us by one language, the sacred language of a great people's creative endeavour.

People who could erect a building like this in a few months were no icons or miniatures, high reliefs or engravings! They were people like you and I! And it was no longer stones that appealed to us and told us their history, but people who had laid them, cut them, carried them over to the building site.

Their love of their country and hatred of the enemy bring them near to the Soviet people. Archaisms of all sorts, stylization, the museum approach—all these take a hurried flight before the elements through which the main, the only, the unswerving patriotic theme of our film can find its fullest expression.

Hence the interpretation of the epithet "saint."** The simplest thing

---

* A church famous for its frescoes. Built in 1198.—*Ed.*

** Alexander Nevsky, Prince of Novgorod, was canonized by the Orthodox Church.—*Author's Note.*

39

would have been to disregard it altogether and leave it to the priests. But that would have been an unsatisfactory conclusion. We decided we could correctly decipher his "saintliness" and I think we have succeeded. Why was Alexander called a "saint"? (I don't mean by the Church but by people. Andrei Bogolyubsky* was named a saint for his martyrdom at the hands of his murderers. But Alexander was no martyr, he was not murdered. Why was he a "saint" then?

Let us be clear about the meaning of the word. In those days the title was the *highest possible appreciation* of merits, such merits for which usual epithets like "brave," "dashing" and "wise" were insufficient.

"Saint!" It is not a matter of the ecclesiastic meaning of the epithet, which the clerics have exploited for ages.

The gist of the matter lies in the true popular love and veneration which surround the name of Alexander Nevsky to this day. In this sense the epithet is highly revealing. It shows that that hero and man of genius saw far ahead of what he was doing: he saw Russia great and unified. And the people felt it in the commanding personality of Alexander Nevsky. It was not accidental that centuries later Peter the Great who was completing the work of the far-sighted ruler of the thirteenth century, had Alexander's remains brought to the site where he intended to build St. Petersburg, thus emphasizing his solidarity with Alexander's line.

In this way the historical interpretation of our main theme deprived the concept "saintliness" of its ambiguous halo, leaving in the hero's character only that obsession with the idea of making his country mighty and independent which burned in his heart.

In this way the dominant trait of our character became clear to us. Two or three additional touches from the chronicles completed his image. The most fascinating quality which the chronicles had passed down to us was that Alexander's triumphs did not turn his head and that he was able to restrain the adoring crowds with stern words of warning. This made him human, brought him still closer to living men. The charm and talent of Cherkasov did the rest.

Fire kept in check by wisdom, a synthesis of the two seemed to be Alexander's another important trait. This synthesis was emphasized

* I.e., God-loving:—*Tr.*

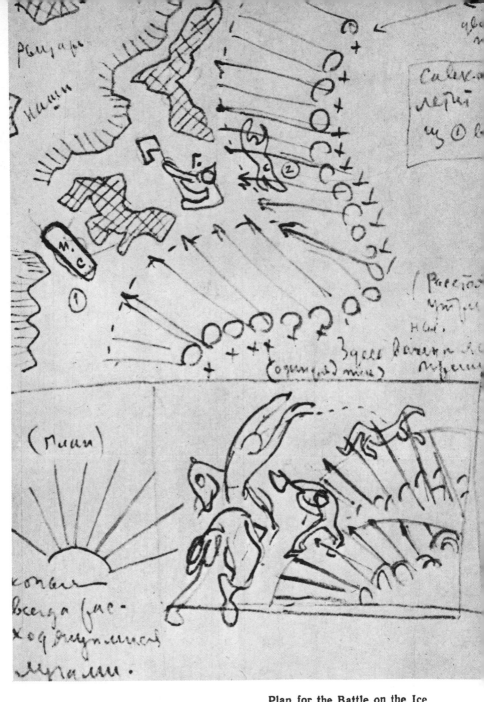

Plan for the Battle on the Ice

Filming the Battle on the Ice (summer 1938)

by the characters of two of his close associates. The name of one of them is known from the chronicles of the Neva Victory; the other was a fictitious character, we may say, a descendant of a hero of any Novgorod epos.

The boldness of Buslai and the wisdom of Gavrilo stand on the right and left of Alexander who possesses both these qualities. The wise Prince knows how to refrain from abusing them and how to put them to good use for the common good. And the two men endowed with these characteristics so typical of Russian warriors displayed their courage—each in his own way—during the Battle on the Ice. A third character, Ignat the armourer, a thorough civilian, is also very much like them. He embodies the patriotic feelings of Novgorod craftsmen. Patriotism is the theme of the film.

Ice-covered Lake Chudskoye. What vastness! What boundless scope! How many temptations it offers to screen Russian winter, crystal-like ice, snow-storms, traces on the snow, hoar-frosted beards and moustaches!... Frozen almost to death on the ice of Lake Ilmen (during our trip to Novgorod in the winter of 1938) we could hardly move our benumbed fingers to note down the effects produced by the boundless expanse of ice and snow clouds.

But there was some delay with the scenario and the only way out was to postpone shooting the winter scenes on location (they took up about sixty per cent of the entire film) to the winter of 1939. Or ... or follow the daring advice of director D. Vasilyev, a new member of our unit, and film winter in summer. Anxiously weighing the pros and cons, I again faced the alternative: real ice or real valour of the Russians? A magnificent symphony of ice brilliantly photographed by Eduard Tisse—next year—or the effective patriotic weapon of a finished film—now? And the aesthetic ice and snow melted. The apple-trees in the back gardens of Potylikha, near the Mosfilm Studios, were transplanted elsewhere, roots and all, the ground was covered with a thick layer of chalk and liquid glass, and the venue was ready for the Battle on the Ice scene. The aesthetic refinement of our former works gave place to the political urgency of the theme.

The artificial winter was a success, complete and indisputable. No one saw the difference.

The reason we succeeded was because we did not try to imitate winter. We told no "lies" and did not try to fool the public with glass icicles and "prop" details of the Russian winter, which cannot be copied faithfully. What we took was the most important aspect of winter—its proportions of light and sound, the whiteness of the ground and the darkness of the sky. We took the winter formula, so we had no need to lie, for the formula corresponded to the truth. We did one more thing: bearing in mind the purpose of the film, we played up the battle, not winter. What we showed was a battle, not the season. Winter was there in a degree making distinction from real winter impossible. In that degree, in that formula of winter relations and in the tact that prompted us "not to show winter" lies the explanation of our success. The considerations which made us "create" winter determined the only correct way of achieving this.

And finally—the time in which we made the film. The time was reduced first by shifting winter to summer and then by thrice advancing our own schedule. This was due to the enthusiasm which the theme aroused in our crew. Curiously enough, unlike my colleagues, *Alexander Nevsky* was my first sound film.

I would have liked very much to experiment at leisure, to try some of the ideas that had haunted me during the years I watched sound films from a distance. But the guns booming at Lake Khasan shattered my intentions. There was no time for day-dreaming. Biting our clenched fists in exasperation that the film was not ready and that we could not hurl it, like a grenade, into the face of the aggressor, we grimly braced ourselves up, and the impossible date of completion—November 7—began taking shape in our minds as something real. I must own that the thought uppermost in my mind to the last day was: "The film cannot be ready by November 7, but ready it *must* be." I wås prepared to face any sacrifice to achieve it: I was willing to give up all that fascinated me in the principles of audio-visual combinations, for it seemed impossible to ensure an organic unity of music and picture in the short time allotted us. It seemed impossible to find and reproduce that wonderful inner synchronization of plastic and musical images, that is, achieve that in which actually lies the secret of audio-visual impression. All this requires time, thinking, cutting and recutting, not once, but many times. Would the image suggest the music? How, or rather when, should I be able to fuse these two elements into one whole?

This is where the magician Sergei Prokofiev came to my rescue.

How did this amazing master capture the inner image of the representation, how did he contrive to discover in a roughly cut scene the logic of its composition, how did he find appropriate musical images for all he saw, how did he find time to score his music for the orchestra with such an astounding effect, and, moreover, work for hours together with our ace sound engineer Volsky and operator Bogdankevich to produce a sound track with a multi-microphone method never used before in our studio?

There was very little time at our disposal. But, however fast the work was progressing, Fira Tobak, my wonderful long-time montage assistant, and I always had the material for the audio-visual combinations ready at hand.

There was very little time at our disposal, but there was no need to make sacrifices: in all important sequences the audio-visual combinations were brought to a level of perfection which could not have been surpassed had we had twice as much time to work on them. We have Prokofiev to thank for this, for his is a combination of a brilliant talent, an unheard-of level of professionalism and ability to develop a terrific tempo.

In this he is a match for our large crew and for the studio as a whole whose energy and enthusiasm alone made it possible to fulfil such an enormous task in so short a time.

Our theme was patriotism.

Whether we have tackled it successfully is for the Soviet audiences to say.

1939

TRUE WAYS OF INVENTION

(Alexander Nevsky)

There is a charming character in *Alexander Nevsky*—Ignat the armourer.

It would have been quite natural to include a craftsman in the original pattern of characters representing the thirteenth-century Russia in all her diversity.

Perhaps the sociological list Pavlenko* and I drew *a priori* did contain such a character. *I don't remember.* But if it did, this character must have been so abstract that it left no trace in my memory. That would have been impossible had we dealt with a character that *lived.*

So we may well assume that no such character ever existed, either in reality or in imagination, which comes to one and the same thing—if he only figured in the rough scenario as a "possibility."

Be that as it may, here is how Ignat was born.

Athena is said to have sprung from the head of Jupiter. The same applies to Ignat the armourer.

With the difference that he sprang from the head of ... Alexander.

Or rather not so much from his head as from his strategic ideas.

I was all for presenting Alexander as a genius. When we speak of genius we always think (and quite correctly!) about something like the apple of Newton or the bobbing lid of Faraday's kettle.

This is quite correct, because the ability to discover in a particular phenomenon a general law and bend this law to the service of man in different spheres of life is certainly a trait to be found in the intricate mental apparatus we call genius.

In everyday life, in practical experience, we define genius simply as an ability to apply deductions drawn from minor chance instances to unexpected major phenomena.

The law of gravity explains why one material particle, say a falling apple, tends to move towards another, say the earth.

If the hero in the film is shown dealing with something like this, the spectators automatically associate it with the notion "genius."

And Prince Alexander appears with the halo of genius surrounding his head.

The film offered him only one opportunity of displaying his genius—through the strategic plan of the Battle on the Ice. This plan was famous for the "pincer movement" which proved fatal for the Teutonic Knights' iron wedge, the "pincer movement" ensuring the complete encirclement of the enemy—something generals of all times have always dreamed of. Besides Alexander, the smashing with "pincers" brought glory to Hannibal, who was the first ever to employ it—in the Battle

---

* Pavlenko, P. A. (1899-1951), a Soviet writer; the script of *Alexander Nevsky* was written jointly by him and Eisenstein.—*Ed.*

of Cannae, and still greater glory to the commanders of the Red Army, who employed it even more brilliantly in the Stalingrad Battle.

We saw clearly what we had to show in the film. We had to show a "Newton's apple" which would suggest to Alexander, as he planned the battle, the strategic picture of the Battle on the Ice.

Such situations are extremely difficult to invent. The hardest thing is to invent an image when you have an almost mathematically precise formula of "what is demanded of it." Take the formula and make an image of it.

There is a more organic and effective process—it is when you simultaneously live through the theme in your imagination and gradually crystallize the formula of the concept (thesis).

But when you have a well-rounded formula, it is very hard indeed to dip it again in the cauldron where initial, "inspired," emotional sensations are brewing.

This has been the stumbling-block for many dramatists and authors, past and present, who have had to deal with plays "with a problem," plays *à thèse,* plays in which actors' performances and the destinies of the characters must show an *a priori* thesis, a formula, instead of allowing the thesis to take shape as the general idea develops, in the *life* process of the work. In the latter case, the thesis will appear as the most pointed statement of the general theme, of the idea that has given birth to the work; in the former case, there are apt to be doubtful "finds" of a purely mechanical nature. But we had no alternative: we were confronted with the necessity of dealing with a case where the "demand" anticipated the development of the scene directly from inner urge—by-passing all formulas—into an image.

No, we had no alternative!

We had to find a solution, to experiment and engage in a play of "offer and choice," in which it was almost impossible to control the "team of two horses"—consciousness and imagination—with one tightly stretched bridle, and make them carry us at a level pace to the common goal—the wise imagery of the whole.

So we began to rack our brain searching and trying....

What did Alexander see on the eve of the battle that suggested to him the best strategic plan for routing the Germans?

The plan itself was known to us.

It consisted in preventing the wedge from cutting into the Russian formation; in getting it stuck and in surrounding it; and in killing, killing, killing the enemy. The wedge. The wedge gets stuck.

Pavlenko immediately pictured night, camp-fires, firewood, chopped, of course.

In chopping wood, the axe got stuck in a knot. The wedge-shaped axe got stuck....

A good beginning but there the imagination trickled out. All this was too wan. No colour in it. Not plausible: can you imagine a forest camp-fire built of even-sized *billets*, like those with which we fed the tile stove in Pavlenko's apartment in one of the wings of the house once occupied (so runs the legend) by the Rostovs and now by the Union of Soviet Writers? In that very wing to which the wounded Andrei Bolkonsky* was brought.

Both of us felt ashamed and began lying to each other: one of us had just remembered somebody was waiting for him and the other that he had an urgent call to make. The next day neither so much as mentioned billets.

Perhaps it was not the wedge Alexander was thinking of but the ice, that it was too thin for the heavy armour-clad knights. (Alexander did take that into account. The ice actually gave way as the knights stampeded in panic and retreated *en masse* to the high bank of Lake Chudskoye).

Well, we might think of that....

The image materialized immediately. The edge of the ice-covered lake and ... a cat treading on it.

The ice was thin at the edge.

The ice ... broke ... under the weight of the cat.

The stupidity of our reasoning was unbearable.

Pavlenko again remembered that somebody was waiting for him and so did I.

Several days passed.

No changes; I don't know about Pavlenko but as for myself, I couldn't sleep.

I imagined axes stuck in billets and cats falling through thin ice, then axes breaking ice, and cats stuck in billets.

* The Rostovs and Andrei Bolkonsky are characters in Lev Tolstoi's *War and Peace.—Ed.*

What silly rot!

There is no telling what comes into your head when you toss in your bed and sleep just won't come.

I reached for a book—anything to occupy my mind.

The book was a collection of old *risqué* Russian folk-tales.

One of the first was "The Hare and the Vixen."

Good God!

How could I have forgotten one of my favourite tales?

I leapt out of bed and rushed to the telephone.

"I've got it!" I roared excitedly.

We would get someone at the camp-fire to tell this tale.

"The Hare and the Vixen."

How the hare slipped through between two birch-trees. How the vixen pursuing him got stuck between the birches.

After half an hour's effort the tale took the shape in which it is told by Ignat in the film.

"So the hare hopped into a ravine and so did the vixen, the hare ran to a copse, and the vixen followed him. Then the hare made for a slit between two birch-trees. The vixen ran after him and got stuck. She got stuck good and well and no matter how she tried to free herself, she couldn't. The hare came up from behind and grimly said, 'Better say bye-bye to your maidenhood.' "

The warriors around the camp-fire would roar with laughter.

And Ignat would go on, " 'Don't, neighbour, please don't. I'll die of shame. Have pity!' 'I've no time for pity,' the hare replied. And he promptly did what he had threatened."

Alexander would hear Ignat telling the tale. (It was a good idea to show the close contact existing between the Prince and his warriors).

He would ask:

"So he got her stuck between two birches, eh?"

"And he did what he had threatened," the reply would come amid loud guffaws.

By that time Alexander's mind would be working out a plan for the complete encirclement of the Teuton horde.

It was certainly not from the tale that his wise strategic move originated.

But the graphic picture of the folk-tale gave him a valuable hint as he planned the arrangement of his troops.

Buslai would let the Teutons' "thin edge" through.

The wedge would get stuck.

And Gavrilo Olexich would press it from the flanks.

While from the rear it would be attacked ... by the peasant militia.

Inspired, brief, exact and at the same time complete in all its details was Alexander's plan for the battle.

We would have Alexander turn to the warriors and say:

"We'll fight on the ice."

And add to Gavrilo and Buslai:

"We'll place our vanguard here, at the Raven Rock. You will lead the left-hand regiments, Gavrilo. I myself will lead the right-hand and the main regiment. You, Mikula, lead your muzhiks from an ambush. The Germans are sure to attack in a wedge, so let the vanguard take the blow upon itself here, at the Raven Rock."

Buslai:

"Who'll lead the vanguard?"

Alexander:

"You. You've been running about all night, now you'll have to stand firm for a day. You'll have to bear the whole brunt of the attack and keep the Germans busy and you mustn't give way while Mikula and I encircle them from right and left. Clear? Let's go!"

And Alexander walked away.

The pleasure of finding the needed image was so great that I almost completely missed the general lesson to be drawn from the experience.

We could achieve nothing while we sought to substitute plastic prototypes, such as the cat, billets, etc., for the plastic image of battle

Then came a suggestion from material of another plane—a tale, a story.

There must be some law or other for this. The suggestion must come from the dynamic scheme underlying facts or objects, not from details themselves.

And if the facts or objects belong to a different plane, say, to the plane of sound and not plastics, the sensation produced by the dynamic scheme becomes more poignant, the mind capable of transplanting it into another plane must be sharp and the effect becomes many times stronger.

But there was no time for meditation.

We had to finish our film script.

The first conclusion I drew from the new solution was that I should place an order with the costume department.

In order to impress on the audience's consciousness the connection between the plan of the battle and the tale, the muzhiks—the peasant militia—striking at the Germans from the rear, would wear big hats made of hare skin.

But it was in another direction that the "chain reaction" of invention was developing with particular momentum, namely, in the direction of detailed development of the story-teller's image. We needed a very good actor for the role. Which of our actors was the best story-teller?

Dmitry Nikolayevich Orlov, of course. People who had heard him read *Dogady* were sure of that. Orlov knew how to convey the wisdom, wilfulness, seeming naïveté and cunning typical of the Russian peasant, workman or craftsman.

Hold everything!

There was a "vacancy" of just this type in the list of characters we wanted to have in the film.

It was no more than a vacancy which had no human features. And yet it had—it was a crop-eared figure copied from the Korsun Gate of St. Sophia's Cathedral in Novgorod.

The nature of the tale and the cunningly insinuating wink of Orlov, would make the "representative of Novgorod craftsmen," included in the list of characters under the general heading of *desiderata*, a real, live person.

Orlov would become an armourer.

A wiser man than the young rank-and-file warriors around him.

And it would be natural for him to teach them wisdom by telling them *risqué* tales and allegories.

We should see to it that the tale does not clash with the general style of his conversation and make him speak in saws and proverbs.

And if the tale was to be *risqué* only in form but not in essence, Ignat (the name came of itself) had to be shown as a true Russian and a patriot.

So, in the Town Square scene showing people discussing whether they should fight for "some united Russia" and the propertied classes of Novgorod displaying reluctance to support the common cause, we would have Ignat call on the people of Novgorod to take up arms against the Germans.

There we would have him addressing the people.

Not to make him appear an idle prattler, we had to present him as a patriot not only in words but in deed, too.

We would put him in charge of a whole army of Novgorod armourers forging swords, chain mails and spears night and day. But we would make him active not only in his professional capacity.

We would make him big-hearted.

We would give away all he had forged: "Come and take it all!" But this should not be made to look like a fine theatrical gesture. And so we tinged the character with a bit of irony by making him constantly use bywords and proverbs.

We let him overdo things in his zeal.

We let the armourer give away all the armour he had forged, remaining himself without a mail. ("An armourer without armour"— a new version of the Russian saying "The shoemaker is the worst shod.")

We couldn't let Ignat be that. We had profited by the lesson in "transplanting" situations—remember the cat falling through the ice?

That would have been too much.

We'd leave him without a mail. Still better, we'd make him look a bit ridiculous, wearing a coat of mail *too short for him.*

"The mail's a bit too short," he would say somewhat puzzled, a little saddened and perplexed at finding himself in undersized armour after he had given everything away.

At this juncture the laws of dramaturgy demanded that we should make the spectators hate the enemy still more fiercely.

To do that it was necessary to have one of the heroes killed.

The people killed in the scenes showing the destruction of Pskov were those who had not earned the audiences' sympathies, except that they were their countrymen, men of the same stock—Russians from Pskov.

The Pskov catastrophe was not sufficiently linked with the fate of the characters whom the audiences knew and loved. The words "The mail's a bit too short" sounded well ... so well that we would like to use them several times.

Scene from *Alexander Nevsky*

Between shots (*Alexander Nevsky*)

Between shots (*Alexander Nevsky*)

To make them a kind of refrain.

And a refrain must be presented each time in a new light, with a new meaning.

There we were: we had the refrain, "The mail's a bit too short," on the one hand, and the necessity of having one of the heroes killed, on the other.

We couldn't afford killing Alexander.

Nor Buslai.

Gavrilo Olexich almost died as it was.

Both of them, however, had to remain alive for the final scene.

"The mail's a bit too short."

But a coat of mail could be "too short" not only at the bottom.

It might be too short to protect the throat.

And the ridiculous might become tragic. Coming after the ridiculous, the tragic would ring all the more sadly, and sadness would engender hate for those who had caused it.

So the funny mail, first hesitatingly and then with dramaturgic insistence, offered its "too short" collar to the murderer's dagger. Who was to be the murderer?

The meanest among the enemies, of course—the traitor Tverdila!

Heard for the second time—as the refrain—the words "The mail's a bit too short" would be uttered with the last breath of the lovable man—a gay, cunning, devoted son of his country, an ardent patriot and a martyr for the people's cause.

That was how, in an organic way, there arose the living traits of a new character in a work of art, in just the same way as the really unique and historical event called to life, to deeds and action the heroic people, whose hearts of true patriots prompted them to perform acts which had covered their own names and the people who gave them birth with undying glory.

And there was Orlov moving on the vast Mosfilm lot, enacting one episode after another of the dramatic story of his hero, the armourer, and reaching now and again for a greasy scroll tucked away in Ignat's boot—the thews and sinews of the role—the bywords and proverbs he had to speak.

Each time Orlov bent down he added a new proverb to the list.

Perhaps it might be useful.

A saying he had read somewhere.

And suddenly remembered. Or heard someone say. Or he bent to peruse the scroll and introduce one of the proverbs into his lines, having found a proper place for it....

So it went, with Orlov grunting as he reached for his boot, arguing under his breath with his Ignat about where to use some byword.

He liked the job and never seemed tired of it.

What a pity, Dmitry Nikolayevich, that it's only now that I have happened to see a very colourful proverb. I can well imagine how you'd have said it.

Too late now.

After all, it's eight years since we finished the film....*

1946

---

* The MS ends at this.—*Ed.*

PROBLEMS OF FILM DIRECTION

ORGANIC UNITY AND PATHOS*
IN THE COMPOSITION OF POTEMKIN

When *Potemkin* is discussed two of its features are commonly noted: the organic unity of its composition as a whole and the pathos of the film.

Taking these two most characteristic features of *Potemkin*, let us analyze by what means they were achieved, primarily in the field of composition. We shall study the first feature in the composition of the film as a whole. For the second, we shall take the episode of the Odessa steps, where the pathos of the film reaches its climax, and then we shall apply our conclusions to the whole.

We shall concern ourselves with the compositional means employed to ensure these qualities. In the same way we could study other factors; we could examine the contribution to organic unity and pathos made by the actors' performances, by the treatment of the story, by the

* The word is used here in its original sense.—*Tr.*

light and colour scale of the photography, by the natural backgrounds, by the mass scenes, etc. But here we shall confine ourselves to one particular problem, that of *structure*, and shall not attempt an exhaustive analysis of all the film's aspects.

And yet, in an organic work of art, elements that nourish the work as a whole pervade all the features composing this work. A unified canon pierces not only the whole and each of its parts, but also each element that is called to participate in the work of composition. One and the same principle will feed any element, appearing in each in a qualitatively different form. Only in this case are we justified in considering a work of art organic, the notion "organism" being used in the sense in which Engels spoke of it in his *Dialectics of Nature:* "The organism is certainly a *higher unity*."

This brings us to the first item of our analysis—the organic unity of the composition of *Potemkin*.

Let us approach this problem from the premise that the organic unity of a work of art and the sensation of unity can be attained only if the law of building the work answers the law of structure in natural organic phenomena, of which Lenin said that "the particular does not exist outside that relationship which leads to the general. The general exists only in the particular, through the particular."

The first analysis will provide material for the study of laws governing unity in static conditions; the second will enable us to study the dynamic operation of these laws. Thus, in the first instance we shall deal with parts and *proportions* in the structure of the work. In the second—with the *movement* of the structure of the work.

Outwardly, *Potemkin* is a chronicle of events but it impresses the spectators as a drama.

The secret of this effect lies in the plot which is built up in accordance with the laws of austere composition of tragedy in its traditional five-act form.

The events, first taken as unembellished facts, are divided into five tragic acts, the facts themselves so arranged as to form a consecutive whole, closely conforming to the requirements of classical tragedy: a third act distinct from the second, a fifth distinct from the first, and so on.

This age-honoured structure of tragedy is further stressed by the subtitle each "act" is preceded by.

Here are the five acts:

I. *Men and Maggots*

Exposition of the action. The conditions aboard the battleship. Meat teeming with maggots. Unrest among the sailors.

II. *Drama on the Quarter-Deck*

"All hands on deck!" The sailors' refusal to eat the maggoty soup. The tarpaulin scene. "Brothers!" Refusal to fire. Mutiny. Revenge on the officers.

III. *The Dead Cries Out*

Mist. Vakulinchuk's body in the Odessa port. Mourning over the body. Meeting. Raising the red flag.

IV. *The Odessa Steps*

Fraternization of shore and battleship. Yawls with provisions. Shooting on the Odessa steps.

V. *Meeting the Squadron*

Night of expectation. Meeting the squadron. Engines. "Brothers!" The squadron refuses to fire.

The action in each part is different, but they are permeated and cemented, as it were, by the method of double repetition.

In "Drama on the Quarter-Deck" a handful of mutinous sailors—part of the battleship's crew—cry, "Brothers!" to the firing squad. The rifles are lowered. The whole of the crew joins the rebels.

In "Meeting the Squadron" the mutinous ship—part of the navy—throws the cry "Brothers!" to the crews of the Admiral's squadron. And the guns trained on the *Potemkin* are lowered. The whole of the fleet is at one with the *Potemkin*.

From a particle of the battleship's organism to the organism as a whole; from a particle of the navy's organism—the battleship—to the navy's organism as a whole. This is how the feeling of revolutionary brotherhood develops thematically; and the composition of the work on the subject of the brotherhood of toilers and of revolution develops parallel with it.

Over the heads of censors the film spreads in bourgeois countries the idea of the brotherhood of toilers, carrying to them the brotherly "Hurrah!"—just as in the film itself the idea of revolutionary brotherhood spreads from the rebellious ship to the shore.

As far as emotional impact and idea are concerned, that alone would be enough to make the film an organic whole, but we would like to test its structure from the standpoint of form.

In its five parts, tied with the general thematic line, there is otherwise little that is similar externally. Structurally, though, they are perfectly *identical* in that each act is clearly divided into two almost equal parts, this division becoming more pronounced in part II.

The tarpaulin scene—mutiny.

Mourning for Vakulinchuk—meeting of indignant protest.

Fraternizing—shooting.

Anxiously awaiting the squadron—triumph.

Moreover, every "transition" point is emphasized by a pause, a *caesura.*

In part III this is a few shots of clenched fists, showing the transition from grief for the slain comrade to infuriated protest.

In part IV this is the title "Suddenly," cutting short the fraternization scene and ushering in the shooting scene.

In part II this is the motionless rifle muzzles; in part V—the gaping mouths of the guns and the exclamation "Brothers!" breaking the dead silence of expectation and arousing an avalanche of fraternal feelings.

And the remarkable thing about these dividing points is that they mark not merely a transition to a merely *different* mood, to a merely *different* rhythm, to a merely *different* event, but show each time that the transition is to a sharply opposite quality. To say that we have contrasts would not be enough: the image of the same theme is each time presented from the *opposite* point of view, although it *grows out of the theme itself.*

Thus, the rebellion breaks out after the unbearable strain of waiting under the rifles (part II).

The angry protest follows the mass mourning for the slain comrade (part III).

The shooting on the Odessa steps is a natural answer of the reactionaries to the fraternal embraces between the mutinous crew of the *Potemkin* and the population of Odessa (part IV).

The unity of such a canon, recurring in each act of the drama, is very significant.

This unity is characteristic of the *structure* of the *Potemkin* as a whole.

The film in its entirety is also divided near the middle by a dead halt, a *caesura*, when the tempestuous action of the first half is suspended, and the second half begins to gain impetus.

The episode with Vakulinchuk's body and the Odessa mist serves as a similar *caesura* for the film as a whole.

At that point the theme of revolution spreads from one mutinous battleship to Odessa, embracing the whole city topographically opposed to the ship but emotionally at one with it. But at the moment when the theme returns to the sea, the city is separated from it by soldiers (the episode on the steps).

We see that the development of the theme is organic and that the structure of the film born of this thematic development *is identical in the whole as it is in its parts, large and small.*

The law of unity has been observed throughout.

In terms of proportions, organic unity is expressed in what is known in aesthetics as "golden section."

A work of art built on the principle of the golden section is usually most effective.

This principle has been exhaustively applied in the plastic arts.

It is applied less in such arts as music and poetry, although we may safely say that there is a vast field of application in these.

I don't think that a motion picture has ever been subjected to a test on the golden-section principle.

All the more interesting, therefore, is the fact that *Potemkin*, whose organic unity is well known, has been based on this principle.

In speaking about the division of each part of the film and of the film as a whole, we said "two *almost* equal parts." In fact, the proportion is closer to 2:3, which approximates the golden section.

The main *caesura* of the film, the *"zero" point* at which action is suspended, is between the end of part II and the beginning of part III—the 2:3 ratio.

To be more exact, it is *at the end of part II*, for it is there that the theme of dead Vakulinchuk is introduced, and the *caesurae* in the individual parts of the film are likewise shifted. The most astonishing thing about *Potemkin* is that the golden-section principle is observed not only with regard to the *"zero" point* but with regard to the culmination point as well. The latter point is the raising of the red flag on the battleship. This occurs also at a point of the golden section but in *reverse proportion* (3:2), that is, at the point dividing the first three parts from the last two—*at the end of part III*. And the flag still figures at the beginning of part IV.

Thus, we see that each individual part of the film, as well as the film on the whole, its culmination and "zero" points are built strictly in conformity with the principle of golden section, that is, proportionally.

Now let us consider the second distinctive characteristic of *Potemkin*—its pathos and the compositional means by which it is achieved.

We do not intend to define pathos as such. We shall confine ourselves to studying the effect a work marked with pathos produces on the spectator.

Pathos arouses deep emotions and enthusiasm.

To achieve this, such a work must be built throughout on strong explosive action and constant qualitative changes.

One and the same event may be incorporated in a work of art in different guises: in the form of a dispassionate statement or in that of a pathetic hymn. Here we are interested in the means of lifting an event to the heights of pathos.

There is no doubt that the treatment of an event is primarily determined by the author's attitude to the content. But composition, as we understand it, is the means of expressing the author's attitude and influencing the spectators.

That is why in this article we are less concerned with the nature of pathos of one or another event, for this depends on one's social viewpoint. Nor shall we touch upon the nature of *the author's attitude* to this event, for this, too, is determined by his social outlook. What we are interested in is the particular problem of what compositional means are employed to express this attitude within a work of pathos.

Poster for *Potemkin*

Poster for *Potemkin*

If we wish the spectator to experience a maximum emotional up-surge, to send him into ecstasy, we must offer him a suitable "formula" which will eventually excite the desirable emotions in him.

The simplest method is to present on the screen a human being in a state of ecstasy, that is, a character who is gripped by some emotion, who is "beside himself."

A more complicated and more effective method is the realization of the main condition of a work of pathos—constant qualitative changes in the action—not through the medium of one character, but through the entire environment. In other words, when everything around him is also "beside itself." A classical example of this method is the storm raging in the breast of King Lear and everywhere around him in nature.

To return to our example—the Odessa steps.

How are the events arranged and presented in this scene?

Leaving aside the frenzied state of the characters and masses in the scene, let us see how one of the structural and compositional means—*movement*—is used to express mounting emotional intensity.

First, there are *close-ups* of human figures rushing chaotically. Then, *long-shots* of the same scene. The *chaotic movement* is next superseded by shots showing the feet of soldiers as they march *rhythmically* down the steps.

Tempo increases. Rhythm accelerates.

And then, as the *downward* movement reaches its culmination, the movement is suddenly reversed: instead of the headlong rush of the *crowd* down the steps we see the *solitary* figure of a mother carrying her dead son, *slowly* and *solemnly going up* the steps.

Mass. Headlong rush. *Downward.* And all of a sudden—

A *solitary* figure. Slow and solemn. *Going up.* But only for a moment. Then again a *leap in the reverse direction. Downward* movement.

Rhythm accelerates. Tempo increases.

The shot of *the rushing crowd* is suddenly followed by one showing a perambulator hurtling down the steps. This is more than just different tempos. This is a *leap in the method of representation*—from the abstract to the physical. This gives one more aspect of downward movement.

Close-ups, accordingly, give place to *long shots*. The *chaotic* rush (of a mass) is succeeded by the *rhythmic* march of the soldiers. One aspect of movement (people running, falling, tumbling down the steps) gives way to another (rolling perambulator). *Descent* gives place to *ascent. Many* volleys of *many* rifles give place to *one* shot from *one* of the battleship's guns.

At each step there is a leap from one dimension to another, from one quality to another, until, finally, the change affects not one individual episode (the perambulator) but the whole of the method: the risen lions mark the point where the *narrative* turns into a *presentation through images.*

The visible steps of the stairs marking the downward progress of action correspond to steps marking qualitative leaps but proceeding in the opposite direction of mounting intensity.

Thus, the dramatic theme, unfolding impetuously in the scene of shooting on the steps, is at the same time the structural leit-motif, determining the plastic and rhythmical arrangement of the events.

Does the episode on the steps fit in into the organic whole? Does it disrupt the structural conception? No, it does not. The traits characteristic of a work of pathos are given here great prominence, and the episode is the tragic culmination of the entire film.

It would not be out of place to recall what I have said above about the two parts into which each of the five acts is divided in accordance with the golden-section principle. I have stressed repeatedly that action invariably leaps into a new quality at each *caesura*; now I should emphasize that the range of the new quality into which the leap is made is always the *greatest possible*: each time *the leap is into the opposite.*

We see, accordingly, that all the decisive elements of composition conform to the formula of the ecstatic: the action always makes a leap into a new quality, and this new leap is usually a leap into the opposite direction.

In this, as in the case discussed above regarding the principle of golden section and its role of determining proportions, lies the secret of organic unity as manifested in the *development* of the plot. Transition from one quality to another by means of leaps is not merely a formula of *growth* but one of *development.* We are drawn into this development not only as "vegetative" individuals subordinated to the *evolutionary laws of nature*, but as part of collective and social units consciously participating in its development, for we know that such leaps are characteristic of social life. They are the *revolutions* which stimulate social development and social movement.

We can safely say that there is a third aspect of the organic unity of *Potemkin*. The leap which characterizes the structure of each compositional element and the composition of the entire film is the compositional expression of the most important element of the theme—of the revolutionary outburst. And that is one in a series of leaps by means of which social development proceeds uninterruptedly.

The structure of a many-sided work, like that of a work of pathos, can be defined in the following words: a pathetic structure makes us *relive acutely the moments of culmination and substantiation* that are in the canon of all dialectical processes.*

Of all the living beings on earth we are alone privileged to experience and relive, one after another, the moments of the substantiation of the most important achievements in social development. More. We have the privilege of participating collectively in making a new human history.

Living through an historical moment is the culminating point of the pathos of feeling oneself part of the process, of feeling oneself part of the collective waging a fight for a bright future.

Such is pathos in life. And such is its reflection in pathetic works of art. Born of the pathos of the theme, the compositional structure echoes that basic and single law which governs the organic process—social and otherwise—involved in the making of the universe. Participation in this canon (the reflection of which is our consciousness, and its area of application—all our existence) cannot but fill us to the highest point with emotional sensation—pathos.

A question remains: How is the artist to achieve practically these formulas of composition? These compositional formulas are to be found in any fully pathetic work. But they are not achieved by any single compositional scheme determined *a priori*. Skill alone, craftsmanship alone, mastery alone, is not enough.

The work becomes organic and reaches the heights of genuine pathos only when the theme and content and idea of the work become an organic and continuous whole with the ideas, the feelings, with the very breath of the author.

---

* The present article treats of one particular part of these canons. A thorough study of the problem will be dealt with in my forthcoming book for directors.— *Author's Note.*

Then and then only will occur a genuine organic-ness of a work, which enters the circle of natural and social phenomena as a fellow-member with equal rights, as an independent phenomenon.

1939

MONTAGE IN 1938

There was a period in our film art when montage was proclaimed "everything." In the present phase (now ending) montage is denounced as "nothing." Sharing none of these two extreme points of view, we deem it necessary to recall that, along with the other elements cinematography uses to impress the spectator, montage is a necessary part of every work of cinema art. Now that the stormy battle "for" and "against" montage is over, we might as well tackle this problem anew. This is all the more necessary because in the period when montage was "negated" assaults were made at its most unchallengeable aspects which should never and in no circumstances have been attacked. The thing is that in recent years some film producers have so completely "done away with" montage that they have forgotten even its fundamental aim and purpose (which cannot be divorced from the *educational* aim pursued by *every* work of art) —the need for interconnection and sequence in the treatment of the theme, the plot, the action, the movement, both within an episode and within the film as a whole. The result is that there is no logical continuity or *simple narrative*, to say nothing of the *excitement* a story should arouse, in many films of different genres, even in some of those made by outstanding producers. This calls not so much for criticism of the producers as for the restoration of the lost art of montage. And all the more so since our films must be *highly emotional* narratives and not merely *logical exposés* of facts.

Montage is a mighty weapon for achieving this aim.

Why do we use montage in the first place? Even the most fanatical opponent of montage will agree that it is not because we do not have film of infinite length and that we are, therefore, occasionally obliged to stick one short piece to another.

The "Leftists" in matters of montage went to another extreme: while handling pieces of film, they discovered a certain property of montage which so impressed them that they could not shake off the impression for several years afterwards. This property reveals that *any two pieces of a film stuck together inevitably combine to create a new concept, a new quality born of that juxtaposition.*

This is by no means a specifically cinematographic phenomenon, but one we invariably come across in all cases when two facts, phenomena, or objects are juxtaposed. When we see two objects placed side by side, we draw certain conclusions almost automatically. Take, for example, *a grave.* Imagine a weeping woman in mourning beside it. And it is almost a sure guess that you will conclude that she is *a widow.* The effect of Ambrose Bierce's anecdote "The Inconsolable Widow" (from his *Fantastic Fables*) is based on this property of our perception. Here is how he told it:

A woman in widow's weeds was weeping upon a grave.

" 'Console yourself, Madam,' said a Sympathetic Stranger. 'Heaven's mercies are infinite. There is another man somewhere, besides your husband, with whom you can still be happy.' 'There was,' she sobbed, 'there was, but this is his grave.' "

The whole effect of the story is built on the long-established premise that a grave and a woman in widow's weeds beside it cannot mean anything but *a widow* weeping for her husband, when in reality the man whose death she bewails was her lover.

This circumstance is often made use of in riddles. Here is an example from folk-lore. "The raven flew while the dog sat on its tail. Is that possible?" Automatically we take the two elements and add them up. The puzzle is usually put in such a way as to imply that the dog was sitting on the raven's tail while in reality *the two actions* are independent of each other: one, the raven was flying; two, the dog was sitting on *its own* tail.

So there is nothing astonishing in the fact that, given two pieces of film following one after the other, the spectator draws a certain conclusion.

I think we should criticize not the facts themselves, nor their originality or commonplaceness, but the conclusions and inferences drawn from them. These we shall criticize and try to correct.

*   *   *

Where were we wrong when we ourselves pointed out that the phenomenon discussed was of indubitable importance for understanding and mastering montage? What was right and what was wrong in our enthusiastic assertions of those days?

What was (and is) right, is that the result of the juxtaposition of two montage pieces is something more like the *product* than the sum. It is so because the result of juxtaposition is always qualitatively (that is, in dimension, or power, if you like) different from each of the components taken separately. If we take our example, then *the woman* is a representation, the *mourning* she wears is a representation; the two things are objectively representable. But *the widow* concept arising from the juxtaposition of these two representations cannot be depicted; it is a new notion, a new concept, a new image.

What was wrong with our old treatment of this indisputable phenomenon?

The mistake lay in overrating the possibilities of juxtaposition and underrating *research into the problem of material* juxtaposed.

My critics were quick to represent this as a lack of interest in *the content* of the pieces of film, identifying *interest in research* in certain fields or aspects of a problem with the *research's attitude* towards the actuality he depicts.

I leave that to their conscience.

As I see it now, I was mostly fascinated by the fact that film strips—no matter how unrelated, and often in spite of that—engendered a "third something" and became correlated when placed side by side at the editor's will.

I was thus carried away by possibilities that were not typical of the conditions of usual film composition and construction.

The treatment of such material and phenomena naturally led me to ponder on the potentialities of juxtaposition. I paid *less attention to analyzing* the nature of the pieces themselves. And even if I had paid more attention to this aspect, it would not have been enough: the practice of paying attention only to the content of single shots has resulted in the decline of montage with all the consequences arising therefrom.

What, then, ought we to have done to reduce the two extreme practices to a norm?

We should have focused our attention on that which determines both the content of every frame and the compositional juxtaposition of these individual contents with one another—that is, on the content of the *whole, the general, the unifying.*

One extreme led us to attaching too much importance to the problems of the technique of composition (montage methods); the other—to the elements of composition (the content of a shot).

We ought to have studied more thoroughly the very nature of this *unifying factor.* Of the factor which, in equal measure in each film, determines both the content of individual shots and the content resulting from *their juxtaposition* in one way or another.

But to do this, the researchers should have concentrated not on paradoxical cases where this whole, general and final comes unexpectedly of itself, but on cases where individual pieces are correlated and where *the whole, general and final* is predetermined and, in its own turn, predetermines the elements and methods of their juxtaposition. Such cases are the normal, generally accepted and widespread. Here the whole appears as "a third something"; but the general picture of how the shot and the montage are determined—the contents of both—will be more graphic and distinct. And it is these latter cases that are typical of cinematography.

When montage is done from this standpoint, the juxtaposed shots become correctly related. Moreover, the nature of montage, far from being divorced from the principles of realistic film-making, acts as one of the most coherent and practical means of realistically presenting the film's content.

What does such conception of montage really give us? In this case, each montage piece is not something unrelated, but becomes a *particular representation* of the general theme which in equal measure runs through all the shot-pieces. The juxtaposition of such particular details in a given montage construction produces that same *whole and general* which has given birth to each of the details, namely, the generalized *image* through which the author (and, after him, the spectator) relives the theme.

And if we *now* examine two pieces of film put side by side, we shall see their juxtaposition in a new light:

Juxtaposed, piece *A* and piece *B*, both taken from among the elements of an unfolding theme, produce an image embodying the content of the theme with utmost vividness.

Expressed in the form of an imperative, with greater precision, this premise will read as follows:

Representation A and *representation B* must be so selected from among all the possible features within the unfolding theme, they must be so chosen as to make their *(theirs,* and not any other elements') *juxtaposition* arouse in the spectator's perception and feelings the most complete possible *image of the theme itself.*

In our discussion of montage we have used two terms—"representation" and "image." A few words to explain their difference as we understand it.

*   *   *

Let us consider an obvious case. Let us take a white average-size disc with a smooth surface, its circumference divided into sixty equal parts. Every fifth division is marked with a figure—from 1 to 12. In the centre of the disc are fixed two revolving metal rods, tapering at their free ends. One of these rods is as long as the radius, the other, somewhat shorter. Let us suppose the longer rod points at the figure 12 and the shorter, consecutively at 1, 2, 3, etc., until it, too, points at 12. This will be a series of *geometrical* representations of the fact that two metal rods successively form angles of 30, 60, 90, etc., degrees, up to 360.

If the disc is supplied with a mechanism evenly moving the metal rods, the geometrical figure on its surface will acquire a special meaning: it will no longer be a mere *representation*, but an *image* of time.

In this case, the representation and the image it calls to mind are so blended that it requires very special circumstances to separate the geometrical position of the hands on the dial from the concept of time. And yet this can happen to any of us, though under unusual circumstances.

Remember Vronsky after Anna Karenina tells him she is expecting a child? The case we are discussing is described at the beginning of Chapter XXIV, Part II:

"When Vronsky looked at his watch on the Karenins' verandah he was so agitated and so preoccupied that he saw the hands and the face of the watch without realizing the time."

He conceived no *image* of time looking at the watch. All he saw was the geometrical representation of the dial and the hands.

We see that even in a simple case of astronomical time—the hour— the representation on the dial is not sufficient. It is not enough just to *see.* Something must happen to what we see before we perceive the image of the hour at which the event is taking place and not a mere geometrical figure. Tolstoi shows us what happens if this process is lacking.

What is this process? The position of the hands on the dial is associated with a host of visions and sensations connected with the hour shown by a figure. Let us take, for instance, the figure 5. In our imagination we associate this figure with various events which usually happen at this hour: tea, the end of the day's work, the rush-hour in the underground, bookshops closing, or twilight so characteristic of this time of day. In any case, we shall automatically recall a series of pictures (representations) of events occurring at 5 p. m. And all these separate pictures go to form the image of 5 p. m.

Such is the process followed minutely and such it is at the stage when we grasp the meaning of figures associated with the images of the different hours of day and night.

Then the laws governing the economy of psychic energy come into play. The process begins to "condense": the intermediate links of the chain drop off and a direct and momentary connection is established between the figure and our perception of time, the hour to which it corresponds. The Vronsky case shows that this connection may be broken by a sharp mental disturbance, and that the representation and the image then become independent of each other.

We are interested in the *complete* process of the birth of the image we have just described. The "mechanism" giving birth to an image interests us because there is a similar "mechanism" *in real life* serving as the prototype of the method of creating images *in art.*

Let us remember, therefore, that between the representation of a certain hour on the clock and our perception of the image of this hour there lies a long chain of representations of the individual and characteristic aspects of the hour. I repeat that our psychology reduces this intermediate chain to the minimum and that we perceive only the beginning and end of the process.

But as soon as we are called upon, for some reason or other, to establish a connection between certain representations and images which they must evoke in our mind and feelings, we are invariably compelled to employ a similar chain of intermediate representations which, collectively, make up the image.

Let us first take an example from life closely related to what we have said above.

Most of New York streets have no names: they are numbered instead. You have Fifth Avenue, Forty-Second street, etc. This method of naming streets confuses the new-comer. We are accustomed to streets having names, this is much easier for us, for the name of a street evokes in our minds its image. In other words, when we pronounce the name, we experience a whole lot of sensations.

I found it very difficult to remember the *images* of New York streets, and, consequently, the streets themselves. Such neutral words as "Forty-Second Street" or "Forty-Fifth Street," did not call to my mind any sensation of the general appearance of the street in question. To help myself, I began to fix in my memory a series of objects characteristic of this or that street, objects that would make my mind respond to the signal "42" in a different way it would to "45." Thus, my memory was cluttered with theatres, movie-houses, shops, characteristic buildings, etc., a complex for each separate street. This process of memorizing consisted of two stages: in the first stage, in reply to the words "Forty-Second Street" my memory *very slowly* unrolled a whole chain of elements characteristic of the street, but I had no concrete picture of the street, because the separate elements would not yet combine into a single image. And it was only in the second stage, when the elements added up into one, that the number "42" *aroused a series of elements too, but not as a chain*; this time it was something unified—the general aspect of the street, its *integrated image*.

It was only then that I could say I really *memorized* the street. The image of the street formed itself in my perception and feelings in exactly the same manner as an integral and unforgettable image gradually emerges from the component elements of a work of art.

In both cases, whether it be the process of memorizing or the process of perceiving a work of art, the canon is the same—the particular enters our consciousness and feelings through the whole, and the whole, *through the image*.

The image penetrates our consciousness and feelings and, through *aggregation*, its every detail is preserved in our sensations and memory *as part of the whole*. This may be a sound image—a rhythmical and melodic sound picture, or it may be a plastic image—a visual combination of various elements of the memorized series.

The series of representations entering our perception, our conscious-ness in some particular way, is retained as an integral image composed of individual elements.

We have seen that memorizing consists of two very important stages: first, the *formation* of the image; second, the *result* of this forma-tion and its significance as a memorizing factor. It is essential for the memory to pay as little attention to the first stage as possible and, pass-ing through the process of formation as quickly as possible, come to the result. That is where life differs from art. We distinctly see how much the emphasis shifts as we turn from reality to art. And it is quite natural that, having the result in view, art uses all its subtle methods in the *process* of achieving it.

From the standpoint of dynamics, a work of art is the process of the birth of an image in the spectator's senses and mind.* This is a trait of any really true-to-life work of art and the feature that distinguishes it from still-born works acquainting the spectator with the results of a past creative process, instead of involving him in the process as it occurs.

This condition holds good always and everywhere, whatever the sphere of art. Similarly, true-to-life acting is not copying the results of feelings, but calling feelings to life, compelling them to develop and overgrow into other feelings, in a word, to *live before the spectator*.

That is why the images of a scene, a sequence, a whole work are not self-subsisting entities, but something that must be called to life and must develop.

Similarly, if a character is to appear alive, it must unfold before the spectator in the course of action and not be presented as a mechanical figure with a fixed characterization.

It is very important for drama that the course of events not only sup-ply the *ideas* about a character, but *shape*, "give image unto" *the character*.

Consequently, in the actual method of creating images, a work of art must reproduce the process through which, *in life itself*, new images are built up in people's consciousness and feelings.

We have used New York streets to illustrate this. And we have every

* We shall later see that this dynamic principle underlies all true-to-life images in the seemingly static art of painting.—*Author's Note.*

right to expect an artist who has to convey a certain image through the representation of a fact to use a method similar to the one I used in assimilating those streets.

We have taken the example of a dial and shown what process leads to the representation of the image of time. To create an image, works of art have to resort to a similar method.

Let us confine ourselves to the clock.

In the case of Vronsky, the geometrical figure of the clock hands did not call to life the image of time. But there are cases when it is important not so much to realize the astronomical fact of *midnight* as to *relive* this hour in all the associations and feelings an author may desire to evoke. This can be the exciting hour of a tryst, the hour of death, the hour of elopement—all this is much more important than a mere indication that it is midnight.

In such cases, the image of midnight, the fateful hour filled with special purport, is perceived *through the representation of twelve strokes.*

Here is an illustrative example, taken from Maupassant's *Bel ami.* It has the additional merit of employing sound. Its still greater merit lies in that, although it is of a purely montage nature, it is rightly treated as a piece of everyday life.

The scene describes Georges Duroy (who already spells his name Du Roy) waiting in a fiacre for Suzanne who has agreed to elope with him at midnight.

Midnight here is least of all an astronomical hour; it is the hour which is to decide all (or almost all) that is at stake: "It is all over. It is a failure. She won't come."

And this is how Maupassant impresses on the reader's consciousness and feelings the image of this hour, how he emphasizes its *significance*, as contrasted to the description of the corresponding time of night.

"He went out towards eleven o'clock, wandered about some time, took a cab and had it drawn up in the Place de la Concorde, by the Ministry of Marine.

"From time to time he struck a match to see the time by his watch. When he saw midnight approaching his impatience became feverish. Every moment he thrust his head out of the window to look.

"A distant clock struck twelve, then another nearer, then two to-

70

gether, then a last one, very far away. When the latter had ceased to sound, he thought, 'It is all over. It is a failure. She won't come.'

"He had made up his mind, however, to wait till daylight. In these matters one must be patient.

"He heard the quarter strike, then the half-hour, then the quarter to, and all the clocks repeated 'one,' as they had announced midnight...."

We see from this example that when Maupassant had to impress on the reader's consciousness and sensations the *emotional* content of midnight, he did not confine himself to merely stating that the clocks struck twelve and then one. He made us live through the sensation of midnight by making different clocks in different places strike twelve. The twelve strokes coming from different parts combined in our perception to produce the general sensation of midnight. The individual representations blended into an image. And this is achieved by strictly montage means.

This is an example of the subtlest use of montage with the sound image of "midnight" presented in a series of pictures from different camera angles: "distant," "nearer," "very far away." The striking of the clocks is given from different distances, just as an object shot from various camera set-ups and repeated consecutively in three different shot-pieces: "long shot," "medium shot" and "distant shot." Maupassant does not pass off these different striking clocks as a naturalist detail of Paris at night: he describes this chorus to depict "the fateful hour" and not merely to inform that it is "12 midnight."

Had Maupassant intended to impart this information he would hardly have had recourse to such elaborate writing. And he would not have been able to produce such strong emotional effect by such simple means if he had not chosen the montage solution for his artistic problem.

When I speak of clocks and hours I invariably recall an instance from my own work. When we were filming *October* in the Winter Palace in 1927, we came across a very interesting old clock. Its main dial was wreathed by small dials showing the time in Paris, London, New York, etc., in addition to the Moscow (or was it Petersburg?—I don't remember now) time on the big dial. The clock impressed itself on my memory and when I was seeking for means to drive home with utmost forcefulness the historic moment of victory and the establishment of Soviet power, the clock suggested a peculiar montage solution: the hour of the downfall of the Provisional Government shown by the Petrograd time was then repeated on the little dials showing the time at that moment in London, Paris, New York, etc. Thus, this epoch-making moment in the history and destinies of mankind was shown by the various dials, uniting people everywhere, as it were, at this moment of the victory of the working class. The idea was further emphasized by the rotating movement of the dial-wreath; it grew faster and faster, visually unifying all the particular indices of time into a plastic notion of the historic hour.

But at this point I clearly hear my inveterate opponents saying: "What about a single unbroken, uncut strip of film containing the performance of an actor? Doesn't his acting make any impression? Isn't the acting of Cherkasov, Okhlopkov, Chirkov, or Sverdlin impressive in itself?" It isn't true that such questions deal a fatal blow to the montage conception. The montage principle is much broader than that. It is wrong to presume that a sequence is montage-less just because an actor plays throughout a piece and the director does not cut it. Absolutely wrong!

You must look for montage elsewhere: *in the acting itself*. Later on we shall speak of the montage character of the actor's "inner technique." Right now we shall let George Arliss, one of the world's greatest stage and screen actors, say a few words about this problem. In his *Autobiography,* he writes:

"I had always believed that for the movies acting must be exaggerated, but I saw in this one flash that restraint was the chief thing that the actor had to learn in transferring his art from the stage to the screen.

"The art of restraint and suggestion on the screen may any time be studied by watching the acting of the inimitable Charlie Chaplin."

Arliss opposes restraint to emphasis (exaggeration). Suggestion is the extent to which, he says, action should be reduced. So he rejects not only exaggeration but even complete action, and advocates suggestion in their stead. And what is suggestion but an element, a detail of an action, a close-up which, juxtaposed with other similar details, determines a whole fragment of the action? With Arliss, then, a continuous piece of acting is nothing but a juxtaposition of similar determining close-ups which, combined, produce an image of the content

Shooting *October (Ten Days That Shook the World)*:
Eduard Tisse before the camera, Eisenstein behind it
(courtesy The Museum of Modern Art/Film Stills Archive)

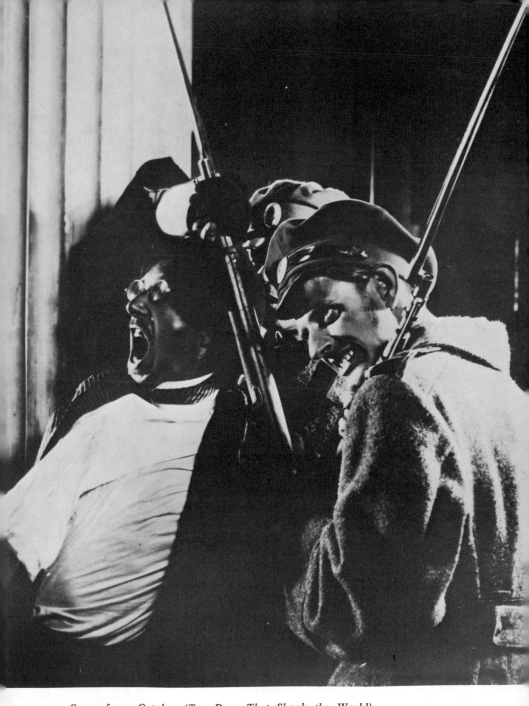

Scene from *October* (*Ten Days That Shook the World*)
(courtesy The Museum of Modern Art/Film Stills Archive)

of acting as opposed to the representation of this content. Accordingly acting can be either flat and representative or truly imagist—that depends on the method the actor uses. Successfully filmed, acting can be truly "montage" by its nature, even when shot from one angle.

The second of the above-mentioned two examples of montage (*October*) is not a usual one while the first (Maupassant) illustrates only a case when one object is shot from different distances and angles.

Here is one more example, this time typical of the cinema and dealing not with an individual object but with the image of an event built up in a similar way.

This example is a wonderful "shooting-script" where an image emerges before our very eyes out of a chaos of individual details and representations. The example is remarkable because it is not a finished work of literature but the notes of a great master in which he wanted to fix for himself the visions he had of the Deluge.

The example in question is Leonardo da Vinci's notes on how the Deluge should be painted. I have chosen the following passage because it gives an extremely vivid visual and auditory picture of the Deluge, a remarkable thing coming from a painter, and yet all the more graphic and impressive.

"Let the dark, gloomy air be seen beaten by the rush of opposing winds wreathed in perpetual rain mingled with hail, and bearing hither and thither a multitude of torn branches of trees mixed together with an infinite number of leaves.

"All around let there be seen ancient trees uprooted and torn in pieces by the fury of the winds.

"You should show how fragments of mountains, which have been already stripped bare by the rushing torrents, fall headlong into these very torrents and choke up the valleys, until the pent-up rivers rise in flood and cover the wide plains and their inhabitants.

"Again there might be seen huddled together on the tops of many of the mountains many different sorts of animals, terrified and subdued at last to a state of tameness, in company with men and women who had fled there with their children.

"And the fields which were covered with water had their waves covered over in great part with tables, bedsteads, boats and various other kinds of rafts, improvised through necessity and fear of death, upon which were men and women with their children, massed to-

73

gether and uttering various cries and lamentations, dismayed by the fury of the winds which were causing the waters to roll over and over in mighty hurricane, bearing with them the bodies of the drowned; and there was no object that floated on the water but was covered with various different animals who had made truce and stood huddled together in terror, among them wolves, foxes, snakes and creatures of every kind, fugitives from death.

"And all the waves that beat against their sides were striking them with repeated blows from the various bodies of the drowned, and the blows were killing those in whom life remained.

"Some groups of men you might have seen with weapons in their hands defending the tiny footholds that remained to them from the lions and wolves and beasts of prey which sought safety there.

"Ah, what dreadful tumults one heard resounding through the gloomy air, smitten by the fury of the thunder and the lightning it flashed forth, which sped through it, bearing ruin, striking down whatever withstood its course!

"Ah, the number of those stopping their ears with their hands in order to shut out the loud uproar caused through the darkened air by the fury of the winds mingled together with the rain, the thunder of the heavens and the raging of the thunderbolts!

"Others were not content to shut their eyes but placing their hands over them, one above the other, would cover them more tightly in order not to see the pitiless slaughter made of the human race by the wrath of God.

"Ah me, how many lamentations!

"How many in their terror flung themselves down from the rocks!

"You might have seen huge branches of the giant oaks laden with men borne along through the air by the fury of the impetuous winds.

"The number of boats capsized and lying, some whole, others broken in pieces, on the top of men struggling to escape with acts and gestures of despair which foretold an awful death!

"Others with frenzied acts were taking their own lives in despair of ever being able to endure such anguish; some of these were flinging themselves down from the lofty rocks; others strangled themselves with their own hands; some seized hold of their own children, and with mighty violence slew them at one blow; some turned their arms

74

against themselves to wound and slay; others falling upon their knees were commending themselves to God.

"Alas! how many mothers were bewailing their drowned sons, holding them upon their knees, lifting up open arms to heaven, and with diverse cries and shrieks declaiming against the anger of the gods!

"Others with hands clenched and fingers locked together gnawed and devoured them with bites that ran blood, crouching down so that their breasts touched their knees in their intense and intolerable agony.

"Herds of animals, such as horses, oxen, goats, sheep, were to be seen already hemmed in by the waters, and left isolated upon the high peaks of the mountains, all huddling together, and those in the middle climbing to the top and treading on the others, and waging fierce battles with each other, and many of them dying of starvation.

"And the birds had already begun to settle upon men and other animals, no longer finding any land left unsubmerged which was not covered with living creatures.

"Already had hunger, the minister of death, taken the lives of a great number of animals; meanwhile dead bodies affected by ferment rose from the depths and beat against each other like so many inflated balls, and rebounded from where they had struck to pile upon the bodies of those just killed.

"And above these horrors the atmosphere was seen covered with murky clouds that were rent by the jagged course of the raging thunderbolts of heaven, which flashed light hither and thither amid the obscurity of the darkness...."

The foregoing was not intended by its author as a poem or literary sketch. Péladen, the editor of the French edition of Leonardo da Vinci's *Trattato della pittura*, regards this description as an unrealized plan of a picture, which would have been an unsurpassed *"chef-d'œuvre* of landscape and the representation of elemental struggles." All the same, the notes are far from being chaotic and, if anything, they accord with the requirements of temporal, rather than the spatial arts.

Without paying a close study to the structure of this remarkable "shooting-script," let us note that the description follows a strictly defined movement. *The course of this movement* is by no means fortuitous. The movement follows a definite order and then, in corresponding reverse order, returns to phenomena matching those of the opening. Beginning with a description of the heavens, the picture ends with it. In the centre is a group of humans and their experiences; the scene develops from the heavens to the humans and back through groups of animals. The most noticeable details (the close-ups) are given in the centre, at the climax of the description ("hands clenched and fingers locked together ... bites that ran blood"). The elements typical of montage composition are clearly defined.

The content within each frame of the separate scenes is enhanced by the increasing intensity of the action.

Let us consider what we may call the "animal theme": animals trying to escape; animals borne by the flood; animals drowning; animals struggling with human beings; animals fighting one another; the carcasses of drowned animals floating on the surface. Or the gradual disappearance of *terra firma* from under the feet of the people, animals and birds, reaching the climax where the birds have to settle on the humans and animals because they can find no tiny bit of land or a branch that is not already occupied. This part of Leonardo da Vinci's notes is an extra reminder of the fact that the distribution of details on the single plane of a picture depends on a compositionally directed movement of the eye from one phenomenon to another. Of course, here this movement is freer than in the cinema where the eye *cannot* discern the succession of the sequence of details in any other order than the one created by the editor.

By his sequential description Leonardo da Vinci, doubtless, wants not merely to enumerate the details but also to trace the trajectory of the future movement of the attention over the surface of the canvas. This is a brilliant example of the fact that in the seemingly static "co-existence" of details in an immobile picture, the same montage selection is applied, the same ordered succession in the juxtaposition of details as in those arts that include the time factor.

Montage performs realist functions in cases where the juxtaposition of individual pieces produces the generality, the synthesis of one's theme, that is, an image embodying the theme.

Having arrived at this definition, let us consider the course of the creative process. The author sees with his mind's eye some image, an emotional embodiment of his theme. His task is to reduce that image to two or three *partial representations* whose combination or juxtaposition shall evoke in the consciousness and feelings of the spectator the same generalized initial image which haunted the author's imagination.

I mean the image of a work as a whole and of each individual scene. All this may be applied in like manner and with as much right to the creation of an image by the actor.

The actor faces a similar task: through two, three, or four traits of a character or of a mode of behaviour to express the chief elements which, juxtaposed, will create the integrated image conceived by the author, the director and the actor himself.

What is this method remarkable for? First and foremost, for its dynamics. For the fact that the desired image is not *ready-made, but arises, comes into virtual being*. The spectator witnesses the birth of an image as conceived by the author, the director and the actor and concretized by them in isolated elements of representation. And that is the ultimate goal and creative aspiration of every actor.

Maxim Gorky vividly expressed this idea in a letter to Konstantin Fedin:

"You say you are worried by the question, 'How to write?' I have been watching for twenty-five years how this question worries people.... Yes, yes, this is a serious question and I was, am and shall be worried by it to the end of my days. To me this question presents itself in the form: 'How must I write to have a man, whoever he may be, emerge from the pages of a story written about him with that almost physical tangibility of his being, with that convincing, *all but fantastic* reality, with which I see and feel him?' That is the core of the matter for me, that is the secret of the problem...."

Montage helps to solve it. The strength of montage lies in that the emotions and minds of the spectators are included in the creative process. The spectator is made to traverse the road of creation which the author traversed in creating the image. The spectator not only sees those elements of the work which are capable of being seen but also experiences the dynamic process of the emergence and formation of the image just as it was experienced by the author. This probably is the highest possible degree of approximation to visually conveying the author's sensations and conception in the greatest possible completeness, to conveying them with "that almost physical tangibility" with which they arose before the author during the creative process, at the moments of his creative vision.

It would be pertinent to give here Marx's definition of the road of genuine investigation:

"Not only the result, but the road to it also, is a part of truth. The investigation of truth must itself be true, true investigation is unfolded truth, the disjointed members of which unite in the result."

This method has one more strong point in that it draws the spectator into a creative act in which his own personality is not dominated by that of the author, but fully develops in harmony with the author's conception, just as the personality of a great actor fuses with that of a great playwright in the process of creating a classical image on the stage. And, indeed, each spectator creates an image along the representational guidance suggested by the author, leading him unswervingly towards knowing and experiencing the theme in accordance with his own personality, in his own individual way, proceeding from his own experience, from his own imagination, from the texture of his associations, from the features of his own character, temper, and social status. The image is at one and the same time the creation of the author and the spectator.

One would say that nothing can be more exact and definite than the almost scientific enumeration of details of the Deluge as given in Leonardo da Vinci's "shooting-script." And yet how highly personal and individual is each of the final images arising before the readers of this list of details that are shared by all. They are at once as similar —or as dissimilar—as the roles of Hamlet or Lear played by actors of different countries, epochs and theatres.

Maupassant offers his readers one montage treatment of striking clocks. He knows that this structure will not only evoke in the minds information of the hour of night but will make the readers appreciate the significance of the hour of midnight. Each reader "hears" the same chimes. But each forms his own image, his own idea of midnight and its significance. All these images and ideas are individual, different, and yet thematically identical. And for each reader-spectator each image of midnight is simultaneously the author's and his own—living and intimate.

The image conceived by the author has become flesh of the flesh of the spectator's risen image. One that was borne by me—the spectator, one that I myself have created. The image is creative not only for the author but also for me, the creative spectator.

At the beginning of the article we spoke of an emotionally exciting and moving story as distinct from a logical exposition of facts—as much difference as there is between an experience and an affidavit.

Non-montage construction in all the above-mentioned instances would be an affidavit exposition. It would be a mere "list" of Leonardo da Vinci but drawn up without regard to the different planes along the preconceived trajectory of the eye over the surface of the future picture. In *October* it would be an immovable dial registering the time of the overthrow of the Provisional Government. In Maupassant's story it would be a brief informative item that the clock had struck twelve. In other words, they would be documents, not raised by artistic means to the heights of true emotional effect. They would all be, in terms of the cinema, *representations shot from a single set-up*, whereas in the form given them by the artists they are images called to life by means of *montage construction*.

And now we can say that it is the *montage* principle, as distinct from one of *representation*, which makes the spectator create and which arouses in him that intensity of inner creative excitement* which distinguishes an emotionally exciting work from the informative logic of a plain statement recording events.

At the same time we discover that in films the montage method is one of the aspects of the application of the *montage principle in general*, a principle which, if understood in this light, goes far beyond the limits of splicing bits of film together.

The best specimens of literature invariably offer us as great a multitude of pictures out of which two or three details are selected with utmost strictness.

*　*　*

* It is quite evident that the *theme as such* can excite emotions irrespective of the way in which it is presented. A short news item about the victory of the Spanish Republicans at Guadalajara excites stronger emotions than a work of Beethoven. But we are discussing here the artistic ways and means of making a theme or subject, by itself capable of exciting emotions, still more impressive. It is also quite clear that montage, as such, is not an exhaustive means in this field, though it is an extremely powerful one.—*Author's Note.*

It was not in vain that we compared the *creative method of the spectator with that of the actor.* For it is here that the montage method enters the least expected sphere—the sphere of the *inner* technique of the actor and of the forms of that *inner process* through which the actor creates a living feeling which enables him to give a realistic performance on the stage or on the screen.

A number of systems and doctrines have been created in the field of acting. Or rather, two or three systems with various offshoots which differ not so much in terminology as—and chiefly—in that the advocates of different trends attach importance to and place emphasis on the *different* main points of acting technique. Sometimes a certain school almost completely loses sight of an entire link in the psychological process of the creation of images; sometimes, on the contrary, too much emphasis is laid on a link of *secondary importance.* Even at the Moscow Art Theatre, with its solid and unified method, there are independent concepts as regards its application.

I shall not delve into either the terminological or essential differences in the methods of the actor's work. I shall touch upon those features of inner technique the main principles of which are the *sine qua non* of the actor's work in all cases when it proves effective, that is, when it grips the spectators. In the final analysis each actor and director can deduce these features from his own "inner" processes if he but stops this process for a moment in order to examine it. The techniques of the *actor* and the *director* in *this* sphere of the problem are inseparable, because to a certain extent a director is also an actor. I shall cite a concrete instance of the "actor's part" in my own directorial experience in order to illustrate the inner technique that is the subject of our study. I must add that the last thing I am aiming at is making any *discoveries* in this field.

Let us suppose that I have to play the part of a man on the morning after he had lost government money at cards. Suppose the scene is full of such varied actions as a conversation with the unsuspecting wife, a scene with the daughter who looks inquiringly at her father, upset by his strange behaviour, fearful expectation of the telephone call that would summon him, the embezzler, to account, and so on.

Let a series of such scenes lead the man to the idea of suicide. The actor has to play the final fragment of the scene in which he becomes convinced that blowing his brains out is the only escape, and his hand begins fumbling almost automatically for his gun in the drawer of his desk.

I don't think there is a cultured actor today who would try to "act the feelings" of a man about to kill himself. Instead of puffing up his emotions and inventing actions, every actor would do something else: he would compel the appropriate consciousness and the appropriate feeling to *take a firm hold* of him. And the vivid feeling, sensation and experience would immediately manifest themselves in correct and emotionally justified movements, actions and general behaviour. That is the way of *establishing the initial elements* of correct behaviour, correct in the sense that it corresponds to a sensation or feeling that has truly been experienced.

The next stage in the actor's work will be the compositional elaboration of these elements, the elimination of all that is accidental, the elevation of these elements to the highest level of expressiveness. But this is the *next* stage, and we are interested in the *preceding* one.

What we are interested in is that stage of the process when the actor becomes possessed by the emotion.

How is this brought about, "how is it done?"

We have said that we will not try to puff up our emotions. Instead, we shall take a road that is known and used by almost everybody.

We shall arouse in our imagination a series of concrete pictures or situations appropriate to our theme. The imagined pictures will fill us with the desired emotion, feeling, sensation, experience. The contents of the imagined pictures will differ, depending on the peculiarities of the image and the character of the man played by the actor.

Suppose that the dominant trait of our embezzler is fear of public opinion. It is not his conscience he dreads most, nor the feeling of guilt, nor the horrible thought of imprisonment, but the thought of *what will people say.*

With such a man, the thing that mostly fills his mind is just these dreadful consequences. And it is these considerations that will bring him to that degree of despair from which there is no escape but death.

This is exactly what takes place in actual life: the fear of responsibility feverishly suggests the consequences and the horrible pictures in turn influence the emotions, intensifying them and driving the embezzler to utter despair.

The process by which the actor brings himself to that emotional

state on the stage is the same. The difference is that here he consciously makes his imagination draw the picture of the consequences which
in life would arise spontaneously.

It is not the aim of this article to discuss how the actor makes his
imagination do this in make-believe circumstances. I am dealing with
the process from the moment the actor's imagination begins to picture
the necessary situations. The actor does not have to make himself feel
and experience the consequences that arise in his imagination, for the
feelings and emotions, as well as the actions they suggest, arise of
themselves, called to life by the pictures drawn by his imagination.
The emotions will be evoked by the pictures themselves, by their combination and juxtaposition. In my search for ways and means of arousing the required feelings, I draw in my imagination a countless number of pictures and situations representing one and the same theme in
various aspects.

Let us take the first two situations that rise before my mind's eye
and put them down just as I see them. "I am a criminal in the eyes of
my former friends and acquaintances. People shun me. I am an out-
cast, etc. . . ." In order to feel all this, I picture concrete situations, real
pictures of what is in store for me. Let the first be a court-room scene
where my case is being heard. Let the second be my return to life
after serving my time in prison.

Let us try to reproduce, in a plastic and graphic form, the numerous
fragmentary situations that our imagination evokes at a moment's notice. Every actor has his own set of such situations.

Here I put down the first things that come to my mind when I set
out to solve this problem.

A court-room. My case is being heard. I am in the dock. The room is
full of people who know or used to know me. I catch the eye of a
neighbour with whom we have lived next door for thirty years. He notices that and with faint indifference looks away and stares absent-
mindedly out of the window. Here is another person—the woman who
lives in the flat above ours. When her gaze meets mine, she lowers her
eyes in alarm but continues to watch me out of the corners of her eyes.
The man I usually played billiards with demonstratively turns his
back on me. And here are the fat owner of the billiards parlour and his
wife arrogantly staring at me with glassy, fish-like eyes. I draw in my
shoulders and look fixedly down. I no longer see anybody but I do

hear whispered accusations and the sibilant sounds of murmuring voices. And the sledge-hammer summing-up speech of the prosecuting attorney.

I can imagine the other scene—my return from prison—just as vividly.

The prison gate shuts with a clang behind me and I am in the street. The maid busy cleaning the window in the house next door pauses in her work and looks questioningly at me as I pass on my way home. There's a new name-plate on the door of my former home. The floor of the hall has been painted anew and the doormat, too, is new. The door of the neighbour's flat opens and unfamiliar faces peer inquisitively at me. Children press against the grown-ups: they are instinctively afraid of me. The old door-man who remembers me as I used to be looks disapprovingly from down stairs, his nose pointed upwards under his awry spectacles. . . . There are three or four time-yellowed letters for me, written before my shame became generally known. . . . Two or three coins jingling in my pocket . . . and then the door of my former acquaintance is shut in my face. . . . My feet carry me hesitantly up the stairs to a friend's, but turn back when there are only two more steps to go. A person I meet recognizes me and turns up the collar of his coat. . . .

That is what swarms in my imagination when I try to experience emotionally a given situation as director or actor.

Imagining myself first in the first situation and then in the second, and calling to mind a few more similar situations, I gradually come to feel what awaits me in the future and then switch to experiencing the tragic hopelessness of my present situation. The juxtaposition of the details of the first situation produces one shade of the emotion. The juxtaposition of the details of the second situation brings about another shade of the same emotion. Three or four shades combine to form a complete image of hopelessness, undistinguishable from the acute emotional sensation of feeling this hopelessness.

In this way, without straining himself in the attempt to portray a feeling, an actor can evoke this feeling through the combination and juxtaposition of deliberately selected details and situations.

It does not matter here whether or not the above-mentioned description of the process is identical to what is taught by the existing schools of acting technique. What does matter is that a phase similar to the one described above invariably attends the process of *shaping and intensifying* emotions, both in actual life and in the technique of the creative process. We can prove this by watching ourselves, whether in the creative process or in actual life.

And the important thing is that creative technique reproduces the process just as it occurs in life, in accordance with the demands peculiar to art.

It is quite clear that we are not dealing with acting technique as a whole but with only a single link of it.

For instance, we have not touched upon the nature of imagination as such, the methods of "awakening" it, or the process it undergoes in creating the mental pictures called for by the theme. Lack of space prevents us from discussing these "links," although were we in a position to do so we would see that these, too, corroborate our ideas. We shall confine ourselves to the one aspect we have discussed, but we must bear in mind that this "link" is of no greater importance in the actor's technique than ... montage in the arsenal of cinematography's expressive means. No greater—and no lesser.

* * *

All this is very well but what is the difference (in practice and in principle) between the inner technique of the actor we have just analyzed and the essence of cinematographic montage we have set down earlier? The difference lies only in the sphere of application and not in the essence of the method.

In the former case we are concerned with arousing living feelings and emotions within the actor.

In the latter—with arousing emotionally experienced images in the mind of the spectator.

In both cases, the juxtaposition of given elements, imagined and static, gives birth to a dynamically emerging emotion, a dynamically emerging image.

We can see, then, that all this does not differ in principle from what we achieve by means of film montage: here we see the emotional theme assuming the same sharp concrete shape through determining details, and the effect resulting from the juxtaposition of details and giving birth to the emotion itself.

As to the nature of these component mental pictures seen by the

Editing *October* (1928)

Sergei Eisenstein conducts a class in film direction at the
State Institute of Cinematography in 1941

actor's "inner eye," their visual (or auditory) essence is absolutely identical to that of film shots. That is why we referred to the pictures above as "fragments" and "details," meaning individual pictures not as a whole but in their most important particulars. For if we attentively examine the almost mechanical recording of the pictures which we tried to fix with the photographic precision of a psychological document, we shall see that the pictures themselves are specifically cinematographic, with camera angles, set-ups at various distances, and rich montage material.

One shot, for example, is chiefly that of a man turning his back, obviously a composition cut by the frame lines of his back rather than of the whole figure. The two heads with bulging eyes staring at me are in contrast with the lowered gaze of my female neighbour watching me out of the corners of her eyes, obviously requiring a distinction in the distance of the camera from the subjects. In another scene the new name-plate on the door and the three letters are typical close-ups. Or take another aspect: the sound long shot of the people whispering in the court-room and the sound close-up of the coins jingling in my pocket, and so on. The mental "lens," too, has its "long shots" and "close-ups," behaving in this respect just like a film camera shooting component pictures within the strictly defined limits of the frame. It is enough to number each of the fragments above to have a typical montage structure.

This reveals the secret of writing shooting-scripts of genuine emotion and interest, and not scripts packed with alternating close-ups, medium shots and long shots!

The basic canon of the method holds good for both spheres. The task is creatively to dissect the theme into its determining representations and then to combine these representations in such a way as to call to life the *initial image of the theme*. The process of the birth of the image in the spectator's mind is inseparable from the experiencing of its content. Just as inseparable from this intense experience is the work of the director, writing his shooting-script. For this is the only path that can lead him to finding the determining representations which will create the live image of the theme in the mind of the spectator.

Therein lies the secret of the emotional narrative (as distinct from factual information) of which we spoke earlier and which is as much a property of a true-to-life performance as it is of live film montage.

The finest literary works invariably contain a similar wealth of pictures, carefully selected and reduced to the extreme laconism of two or three details.

Take, for instance, Pushkin's *Poltava*. There is the scene of Kochubei's execution. In this scene the idea of "Kochubei's end" is expressed with utmost forcefulness through the image of "the end of Kochubei's execution." The image of the execution itself is created by the juxtaposition of three "documentary" representations of the three details characteristic of the end of an execution:

> *"Too late," someone then said to them,*
> *And pointed finger to the field.*
> *There the fatal scaffold was dismantled,*
> *A priest in cassock black was praying,*
> *And on to a wagon was lifted*
> *By two Cossacks an oaken coffin.*

It would be hard to find a more impressive set of details evoking the image of death in all its grimness than in the finale of the execution scene.

We can cite many interesting examples to prove how well this method solves the problem of emotional effect.

Here is another scene from the same poem, where Pushkin magically creates in the reader's mind a vivid and highly emotional image of the elopement:

> *But no one knew just how or when*
> *She vanished. A lone fisherman*
> *In that night heard the clack of horses' hoofs,*
> *Cossack speech and a woman's whisper....*

Here we have three pieces:
1. The clack of horses' hoofs;
2. Cossack speech;
3. A woman's whisper.

Here again three representations objectively expressed (in sound!) combine to create a unifying and emotionally effective image—which would not be the case if each of the three phenomena were taken separately. This method is used with the sole aim of arousing the required emotion in the reader. Yes, an emotion, because the author himself informs the reader of the fact that Maria has vanished. But having revealed her disappearance, the author wants the reader to feel it. To achieve this, he resorts to montage and, giving three details of the elopement, he creates, through montage, the image of the night flight and makes the reader experience it.

To the three sound representations he adds a fourth which serves as a full stop. This fourth representation is taken from another dimension: it is not a sound one but a visual and plastic close-up:

> ... *And eight horseshoes have left their traces*
> *Over the meadow morning dew.* ...

Pushkin thus uses the montage method to create images in his works. He uses the same method in portraying his characters. Superlatively combining various aspects (i. e., camera angles) and different elements (i. e., pieces of things represented in a shot) he creates unbelievably real images. From the pages of Pushkin's poems there emerge real and tangible images of men.

When he has many "pieces" at his disposal, Pushkin carries montage still further. In a montage structure, the rhythm based on the succession of long sentences by sentences limited to one word becomes a means of dynamic characterization. This rhythm seems to emphasize the temperament of the person portrayed, to characterize dynamically his action.

And finally we can learn from Pushkin the order in which to portray and reveal man's image and present his character. In this respect the best example is the description of Peter in *Poltava*.

    I. *...And then with highest exaltation*
   II. *There sounded, ringing, Peter's voice:*
  III. *"To arms, God with us!" From the tent,*
  IV. *By crowding favourites surrounded,*
   V. *Peter emerges. His eyes*
  VI. *Are flashing. His look is terrible.*
 VII. *His movements swift. Magnificent he.*
VIII. *In all his aspect, wrath divine.*
  IX. *He goes. His charger is brought to him.*

X. *Fiery and docile faithful steed.*
XI. *Scenting the fray's fire.*
XII. *It quivers. It turns its eyes aslant*
XIII. *And dashes into the fight's dust,*
XIV. *Proud of its mighty rider.*

The above numbering is of the poem's lines. Let us now write out this same passage again as a shooting-script, numbering the "shots" as edited by Pushkin:

1. And then with highest exaltation there sounded, ringing, Peter's voice: "To arms, God with us!"
2. From the tent, by crowding favourites surrounded,
3. Peter emerges.
4. His eyes are flashing.
5. His look is terrible.
6 His movements swift.
7. Magnificent he.
8. In all his aspect, wrath divine.
9. He goes.
10. His charger is brought to him.
11. Fiery and docile faithful steed.
12. Scenting the fray's fire it quivers.
13. It turns its eyes aslant.
14. And dashes into the fight's dust, proud of its mighty rider.

The number of *lines* and the number of *shots* prove to be *identical,* fourteen in each case. But there is almost no internal congruence between the lay-out of the lines and the lay-out of the shots; such congruence occurs only twice in the entire fourteen lines (VIII-8 and X-11). The content of a "shot" varies from two full lines (1,14) to one word (9).*

This is very instructive for film workers, and particularly those specializing in sound.

Let us analyze the "montage" of Peter's image.

Shots 1, 2 and 3 are a wonderful example of the *significant* presentation of a figure in action. His appearance is described in three stages: 1. We do not see Peter but hear his voice (sound); 2. Peter has emerged from the tent but we cannot see him as he is surrounded

---

* In Russian "he goes" is a single word.—*Tr.*

by a group of favourites; 3. And only in the third piece do we see Peter.

Next come flashing eyes—the determining detail in his portrait (4) and after that his whole face (5). And only after that is his figure (probably down to his knees) shown, perhaps in order to let us see the abruptness and quickness of his movements. The rhythm and characteristics of his movements are expressed by the clash of abrupt short phrases. A full-length portrait is given only in shot 7, and this time the description is colourful (imagist) and not factual: "Magnificent he." In the next shot this general description is emphasized by a concrete metaphor: "In all his aspect, wrath divine." Thus it is only in the eighth shot that Peter stands revealed in all his plastic might. This shot presents a picture of Peter at full height, solved with all the imagist expressive means of shot composition, with a crown of clouds above him, with a tent and people around him and at his feet. And after this broad canvas the poet takes us back to the sphere of movement and action with the laconic "he goes" (9). It would be difficult to capture and present more vividly another of Peter's determining characteristics (along with his "flashing eyes")—his stride. This brief "he goes" fully conveys the impression of the elemental, firm, gigantic stride of Peter which his suite is at enormous pains to keep up with. The painter Valentin Serov has likewise succeeded in capturing that "stride of Peter" in his famous painting of Peter at the construction of St. Petersburg.

I think that the foregoing presentation is a correct film reading of the passage. Firstly, this way of presenting *dramatis personae* is characteristic of Pushkin's style as a whole. (Compare the similar presentation of the ballerina Istomina in *Eugene Onegin*.) Secondly, the order of the words determines with utmost precision the *sequence of appearance* of the elements which finally combine to produce the image of the character and bring out its plasticity.

Shots 2 and 3 would be quite different if instead of:

> *From the tent,*
> *By crowding favourites surrounded,*
> *Peter emerges....*

the text read:

> *...Peter emerges,*
> *By crowding favourites surrounded,*
> *From the tent....*

If this began with Peter's appearance instead of leading us to him, the impression would be entirely different. What we actually have is an example of expressiveness achieved by purely montage ways and means. In each individual case the expressive construction will be different. And the expressive construction itself will in each case determine "the only possible order" of "the only possible words" of which Lev Tolstoi wrote in his *What Is Art?*

The order of the sounds and of Peter's words follows the same structure (shot 1).

The poet does not say:

> *..."To arms, God with us!"*
> *Sounded Peter's voice, ringing,*
> *And with highest exaltation....*

He says instead:

> *And then with highest exaltation*
> *There sounded, ringing, Peter's voice:*
> *"To arms, God with us!"....*

In preserving the expressiveness of his exclamation, we must present it so that first its "exaltation" should be felt, then its "ringing" quality, next the voice should be recognized as belonging to Peter, and finally, the words ("To arms, God with us!") uttered by this exalted, ringing voice of Peter. It is evident that in "staging" this fragment the first two problems could be easily solved if Peter said something first in the tent, perhaps undistinguishable but conveying the exalted and ringing qualities of Peter's voice.

We see that all this is very important for the problem of enriching the expressive resources of film.

The passage above is an example of the extremely complicated auditory and visual composition. One would think that in this field there existed no "visual aids" and that one could gain experience merely by studying the combination of music and action in the opera and ballet.

But Pushkin shows us what we must do to avoid mechanical coincidence between individual visual shots and articulation in the music.

Here we shall discuss the simplest case—non-coincidence between the measures (here—lines) and the ends, beginnings and lengths of the individual plastic pictures. Schematically this can be represented as follows:

Music	I	II	III	IV	V	VI	VII	VIII	IX	X	XI	XII	XIII	XIV
Repre-sentation	1		2		3 4	5	6 7	8	9	10	11	12	13	14

The upper row represents the fourteen lines of the passage and the lower the fourteen representations they evoke.

The diagram shows their relative distribution through the passage.

The diagram clearly shows what exquisite counter-point of the sound-picture elements Pushkin resorts to in order to achieve the wonderful effect in this highly varied passage. Out of the fourteen, only VIII and 8 and X and 11 sections coincide; in the remaining twelve we never come across a single similar combination of verse and corresponding representation.

There is only one instance of complete coincidence of both length and order—VIII and 8. And this is not fortuitous. This single exact correspondence between articulation in music and in representation marks the most important montage-piece in the whole composition. This piece is truly unique: it is that eighth piece in which the image of Peter is revealed in full. This verse gives the only imagist comparison ("In all his aspect, wrath divine"). We see, then, that Pushkin uses coincidence of articulation in music and representation at the most climatic point. An experienced editor, who is a true composer of audio-visual coordinations, would do the same.

In poetry the carrying-over of a picture-phrase from one line to another is called *"enjambement."* In his *Introduction to Metrics*, Zhirmunsky writes:

"When the metrical articulation does not coincide with the syntactic, there arises the so-called carry-over ("enjambement")... . The most characteristic sign of a carry-over is the presence within a line of *syntactic pause* more significant than at the beginning or end of the given line... ."

Or, as one can read in Webster's *Dictionary*: "Enjambement... . Continuation of the sense in a phrase beyond the end of a verse or couplet, the running-over of a sentence from one line into another, so that closely related words fall in different lines... ."

A good example of *enjambement* may be recalled from Keats' *Endymion*:

> ....Thus ended he, and both
> Sat silent: for the maid was very loth
> To answer; feeling well that breathed words
> Would all be lost, unheard, and vain as swords
> Against the enchased crocodile, or leaps
> Of grasshoppers against the sun. She weeps,
> And wonders; struggles to devise some blame
> To put on such a look as would say, 'Shame
> On this poor weakness!' but, for all her strife,
> She could as soon have crush'd away the life
> From a sick dove. At length, to break the pause,
> She said with trembling chance: 'Is this the cause?' ...

Zhirmunsky also speaks of a particular one of the compositional *interpretations* of this type of construction that is also not without a certain interest for our audio-visual coordinations in film, where the picture plays the role of syntactical phrase and the musical construction, the role of rhythmical articulation:

"Any non-coincidence of the syntactic articulation with the metrical is an artistically deliberate dissonance, which reaches its resolution at the point where, after a series of non-coincidences, the syntactic pause at last coincides with the bounds of the rhythmic series."

This can be illustrated by an example, this time from Shelley:

> He ceased, and overcome leant back awhile,
> Then rising, with a melancholy smile
> Went to a sofa, and lay down, and slept

A heavy sleep, and in his dreams he wept
And muttered some familiar name, and we
Wept without shame in his society. . . .*)

In Russian poetry "enjambement" takes on particularly rich forms in the work of Pushkin.

In French poetry the most consistent use of this technique is in the work of Victor Hugo and André Chénier, although the clearest example that I have ever found in French poetry is in a poem by Alfred de Musset:

L'antilope aux yeux bleus, est plus tendre peut-être
Que le roi des forêts ; mais le lion répond
Qu'il n'est pas antilope, et qu'il a nom lion

Enjambement enriches the work of Shakespeare and Milton, reappearing with James Thomson, and with Keats and Shelley. But of course the most interesting poet in this regard is Milton, who greatly influenced Keats and Shelley in their use of this technique.

A close study of such examples and an analysis of the *aims and expressive effects* achieved in each individual case will teach us to arrange audio-visual images in montage.

Poems are usually written in stanzas internally distributed according to metrical articulation—in lines. But there is a powerful poet who writes in a different way—Mayakovsky.

In his "chopped line" articulation is not carried through to accord with the limits of the lines, but with the limits of the "shot." It will be seen that Mayakovsky's breaks are not dictated by the lines:

Emptiness. Wing aloft,
Into the stars carving your way.

but by "shots":

Emptiness.
Wing aloft,
Into the stars carving your way.**

* *Julian and Maddalo.— Tr.*
** *To Sergei Yesenin.—Ed*

He breaks his line just like an experienced editor would in creating a typical scene of collision between stars and Yesenin: first the one, then the other, and then—their collision.

1. *Emptiness.* If this were to be shot, the stars would have to be so presented as to emphasize emptiness and at the same time suggest that they are there.

2. *Wing aloft.*

3. And only in the *third* shot is the meaning of the first and second shots shown in their collision.

Similar carry-overs occur in Griboyedov's *Wit Works Woe.* For instance:

Liza:

> ...*And then, of course, a lump of money,*
> *Enough to cut a dash, give dances—that's his notion.*
> *For instance, Colonel Skalozub, my honey—*
> *A balance at the bank and certain of promotion.*
>
> (Act I).

Chatsky:

> *You don't feel very bright, I see.*
> *Why is it? Is my own arrival not at season?*
> *Or Sophia Pavlovna, may be,*
> *Is she upset for any reason?* (Act II).

But, for an editor, *Wit Works Woe* is interesting yet from another aspect; this interest arises from the comparison of the original MS with different editions. The later editions differ from the earlier not only in text, but, first and foremost, in *punctuation,* with the words and their order remaining unaltered. Punctuation in these editions is often different from that in the *author's original* and a study of punctuation in the early editions is highly instructive from the point of view of montage.

Take the following passage, as it is traditionally printed and read today:

> *They wreck our brains, they empty out our purses;*
> *Creator, save us from these curses,*
> *Their hat-shops, bonnet-shops, their hair-pins, eye-and-hook-shops,*
> *Their cook-shops and their book-shops...*

Originally it was conceived by Griboyedov as follows:

They wreck our brains, they empty out our purses;
Creator, save us from these curses,
Their hat-shops! bonnet-shops! their hair-pins!!

eye-and-hook-shops!!!

Their cook-shops and their book-shops!!!

It is quite clear that in these two cases the passage will be recited differently. And that is not all: if we try to visualize this enumeration in the form of shots, we shall see that the later variant treats the hats, bonnets and pins as something *unified*, that it gives a general representation of all these objects. But Griboyedov's original manuscript presented each of them *in close-up*, in a *montage* of alternating shots.

The two and three exclamation marks are very characteristic. They presuppose, as it were, an increase in the size of the shots. In reciting the verse this is achieved by intonation, by raising one's voice; in the cinema—by a progressive increase in the size of the details.

We are perfectly justified in speaking about the size of *visible* objects. And it does not make any difference that we are not dealing with *descriptive* material as was the case in Pushkin's example. Famusov's words in Griboyedov's example are neither the description of a picture nor the author's presentation of details through which he wishes us to see a character (as we saw, for instance, Peter in *Poltava*). Here we have a series of articles enumerated by a character in a state of indignation. But is there a difference in principle? None whatever! Because in order passionately to denounce all these hats, bonnets and pins, the actor must see them before and around him as he launches into his tirade. He can see them all together—a general view—or in a "montage" sequence—one detail after another. And in increasing size at that, as suggested by the author's two and three exclamation marks. Here the elucidation of whether the objects should be seen all together or in montage shots is no mere pastime: the degree of intonation is determined by the way in which the actor sees these objects. The rise of the voice will not be *artificial*. It will be a natural reaction to the degree of intensity with which he pictures the object.

This passage graphically shows how much more expressive montage construction is when compared with one taken from "a single angle," the way it appears in later editions.

Curiously enough, Griboyedov's comedy abounds in similar examples. The old editions differ from the new ones in that "long shots" are always broken up into "close-ups," and *not vice versa*.

The traditional

> *... To make the whole more eerie,*
> *The floor gapes open, out come you, my dearie,*
> *Quite pale, like death. ...*

is wrong. Griboyedov gives the following:

> *...To make the whole more eerie,*
> *The floor gapes open, out come you, my dearie,*
> *Quite pale! Like death!*

This is still more startling and wonderful in the seemingly simple case of:

> *And every one will call him dangerous conspirer...*

where Griboyedov has:

> *And every one will call him dangerous! conspirer!!*

In both cases we have pure montage. Instead of the inexpressive phrase-picture "quite pale like death" we have two pictures of growing intensity: 1. "Quite pale!" 2. "Like death!" The same applies to the second passage where the theme also grows from piece to piece.

We see that montage was characteristic of the age of Pushkin and Griboyedov. The latter, without resorting to the montage distribution of the lines (as Mayakovsky did), was inwardly akin to the greatest poet of our time.

It is noteworthy that in the sphere of montage Griboyedov's "distorters" proceeded in exactly the opposite way from Mayakovsky. This is what he did in a passage from the poem *Heine-ism* of which we have two variants.

The initial version was:

> *"You are the worst and meanest of all!"*
> *She went and she went on scolding.*

The final version is:

> *"You're worse than the worst,*
> *the worst of all!"*
> *She went*
> *and she went*
> *and she went on scolding.*

The initial version gives two shots at the most, while the final is clearly divided into five. The second line is a "close-up" as compared with the first, and then there are three pieces on one and the same theme in the third, fourth and fifth lines.

So Mayakovsky's poetry is of a graphic montage nature. But for a student of montage Pushkin is of more interest, because he lived in an epoch when "montage" as such was a thing unknown. Mayakovsky, on the other hand, belongs to a period when montage thinking and montage principles were abundantly represented in all arts closely associated with literature—theatre, cinema, photographic montage, etc. Therefore, the examples of strictly realist montage from the *classics* are more piquant, interesting and, perhaps, instructive, because inter-relations in these kindred spheres were either less pronounced or completely absent (the cinema, for example).

Thus, the montage method is apparent everywhere, whether it be in visual, audial or audio-visual combinations, in the creation of an image or situation, or in the "magic" embodiment of a character (in Pushkin's or Mayakovsky's poetry).

What is the conclusion?

The conclusion is that there is no contradiction between the methods employed by a poet, by an actor who *inwardly* embodies what the poet has written, by the same actor performing *within the frame of a single shot*, and by a director who, using the montage method of the exposition and construction of the film as a whole, makes the actor's performance, as well as his environment and all that goes to make the film, sparkle with life. And that is because the methods used by all of them are based in equal degree on live human qualities and principles which are inherent in every human being and every vital art

However diametrically opposite may be these spheres of art, eventually they are bound to become interrelated and unified by the method we now perceive.

These conclusions emphasize once more the necessity for film-makers to study the technique of play-writing and acting and master the finer points of cultured montage craft.

1939

"AN AMERICAN TRAGEDY"*

How an ideological concept works, making a serious approach towards a film, we can trace in my own work which was done in somewhat unusual social circumstances.

It happened in Hollywood, in the world of Paramount Pictures, Inc.**

And the matter concerned the treatment and script of a work of exceptionally high quality.

Although not free from ideological defects, *An American Tragedy* is a first-class work, even though it may not be a class work from our viewpoint. Anyway, it has every chance of being numbered among the classics of its time and place.

That this material offered grounds for a collision of two irreconcilable viewpoints—the "front office's" and ours—became clear the moment we submitted the first rough draft of our script.

"Is Clyde Griffiths guilty or not guilty—in your treatment?" was the first question from the Paramount boss, B. P. Schulberg.

"Not guilty," was our answer.

"But then your script is a monstrous challenge to American society...."

We explained that we considered the crime committed by Griffiths the sum total of those social relations, to whose influence he was sub-

---

* Excerpts from the article "Help Yourself!"—*Ed.*
** During their sojourn in the U.S.A. in 1931-32 S. M. Eisenstein, G. V. Alexandrov and E. K. Tisse consented to make a sound film. Eisenstein and Alexandrov wrote a script but it was rejected. Then they began work on a screen version of T. Dreiser's *An American Tragedy*, but the "front office" disagreed with their treatment. Although Dreiser himself supported Eisenstein the script was turned down.—*Ed.*

jected at every stage of his unfolding biography and character, during the course of the film.

For us, the main attraction of the work lay in that.

"We would prefer a simple, tight whodunit about a murder...."

"... and about the love of a boy and girl," someone added with a sigh.

It should not surprise anyone that it is possible to treat the work's protagonist in two such radically different ways.

Dreiser's novel is as broad and shoreless as the Hudson; it is as immense as life itself, and can be viewed from almost any angle. Like every "neutral" fact of nature itself, his novel is ninety-nine per cent statement of facts and one per cent attitude towards them. This epic of cosmic veracity and objectivity had to be assembled in a tragedy—and this was unthinkable without a world-attitude direction and point.

The studio heads were disturbed by the question of guilt or innocence from another point of view: guilty would mean unattractive. How could they allow a hero to seem unattractive? What would the box-office say?

But if he weren't guilty....

Because of the difficulties around "this damned question" *An American Tragedy* had lain inactive for over five years after its purchase by Paramount. It was approached—but no more than that—even by the patriarch of film, David Wark Griffith, and Lubitsch, and many others.

With their customary cautious prudence the heads, in our case too, dodged a decision. They suggested that we complete the script "as you feel it," and then, "we'll see...."

From what I have said, it must be perfectly clear that in our case, as distinct from previous handlings, the difference of opinion concerned not some particular situation, but had its roots far deeper, touching the question of social treatment wholly and fundamentally.

It is now interesting to trace how a concept adopted in this way begins to determine the modelling of the separate parts and how this particular concept, with its demands, impregnates all problems of determining situations, of psychological deepening, and of the "purely formal" aspect of the construction as a whole—and how it pushes one towards completely new, "purely formal" methods which, when generalized, can be assembled into a new theoretical realization of the guiding disciplines of cinematography.

It would be difficult to set forth here the entire situation of the novel: one can't do in five lines what Dreiser required two bulky volumes to do. We shall touch only upon the outer central point of the outer story side of the tragedy—the murder itself—although the tragedy, of course, is not in this, but in the tragic course pursued by Clyde whom the social structure drives to murder. And it was to this that we drew attention in our script.

Clyde Griffiths seduces a young factory girl employed in the department he manages and cannot help her to an abortion, which to this day is illegal in the U.S.A. He sees himself forced to marry her. Yet this would ruin all his hopes of a career, as it would upset his marriage with a wealthy heiress who is in love with him.

The situation is typical of America, where caste barriers precluding such "mésalliances" are still alien to small-town industrialists. Patriarchal "democratism" still prevails among the fathers who remember the days when, hungry and naked, they came to town to make their fortunes. The next generation brings them closer to the "moneyed aristocracy of Fifth Avenue," and in this respect there is quite a difference in the way Clyde is treated by his uncle and by his cousin.

Clyde is faced with a dilemma: he must either relinquish for ever a career and social success, or get rid of the girl.

Clyde's adventures in his clash with American realities have by this time moulded his psychology so that after a long internal struggle (not with moral principles, but with his own neurasthenic lack of character), he decides on the latter course.

He elaborately plans the murder—a boat is to be upset, apparently accidentally. All the details are thought out with the over-elaboration of the inexperienced criminal, which unavoidably entangles the dilettante in a fatal mesh of incontrovertible evidence.

He sets out with the girl in a boat. In the boat the conflict between pity and aversion for the girl, between his characterless vacillation and his avid desire for a brilliant material future, reaches a climax. Half-consciously, half-unconsciously, gripped by a wild inner panic, Clyde overturns the boat. The girl drowns.

Abandoning her, Clyde saves himself as he had planned beforehand, and falls into the very net that he had woven for his extrication.

The boat episode is effected in the way that similar incidents take place: it is neither fully defined nor completely perceived—it is an un-

Eisenstein in New York (May 1930)

Sergei Eisenstein, Marlene Dietrich and Joseph von Sternberg
(Hollywood, 1930)

differentiated tangle. It is thus "impartially" that Dreiser presents the matter, leaving the further development of events not to the logical course of the story, but to the formal processes of law.

It was imperative for us to stress the *actual* and *formal* innocence of Clyde at the very moment when the crime was perpetrated.

Only in this way could we make quite clear the "monstrous challenge" to a society whose mechanism brings a rather characterless youth to such a predicament and then, invoking morality and justice, seats him in the electric chair.

The sanctity of the *formal* principle in the codes of honour, morality, justice and religion is primary and fundamental in America. On this is based the endless game of the counsels in the courts, and elaborate games among jurists and congressmen. The essence of what is being argued is of minor importance. The issue depends on one's skill in formal argument.

Therefore the conviction of Clyde, though essentially deserved by his role in this affair (which concerns no one) in spite of his *formal* innocence, would be regarded in America as something "monstrous"—a judicial murder.

Such is the shallow but all-pervading and unassailable psychology of the American wherever he may be, and it was not from books that I learned about this side of the American character.

So it was imperative to develop the boat scene with indisputable precision to prove Clyde's *formal* innocence. Yet without whitewashing him in any way, nor absolving him from any blame.

We chose this treatment: Clyde wants to commit the murder, but he *cannot*. At the moment which requires decisive action, he falters. Simply from lack of will.

However, before this inner "defeat," he excites in Roberta such a feeling of alarm that, when he leans towards her, already defeated inwardly and ready "to take everything back," she recoils in horror. The boat, off-balance, rocks. Trying to support Roberta, he accidentally hits her face with his camera, she loses her head and in her terror stumbles, falls, and the boat overturns.

For greater emphasis we show her rising to the surface. We even show Clyde trying to swim to her. But the machinery of crime has been set in motion and continues to its end, even against Clyde's will: Roberta cries out weakly, shrinks in horror from him, and, not knowing how to swim, drowns.

An excellent swimmer, Clyde reaches the shore and, coming to his senses, continues to act according to the fatal plan he had prepared for the crime and which had all but fallen through.

The psychological and tragic deepening of the situation in this form is indubitable. Tragedy is heightened to an almost Grecian level of "blind Moira—fate" that, once conjured into existence, will not relax her hold on the one who dared summon her. It is heightened to racking "causality" that, once it begins to operate, drives on to a logical con-clusion through the pitiless course of its processes.

This crushing of a human being by a "blind" cosmic principle, by the inertia of the progress of laws over which he has no control, con-stitutes one of the basic principles of ancient tragedy. It reflects the passive dependence of the man of that day on the forces of nature. It is analogous to what Engels, in connection with another period, wrote of Calvin: "His predestination doctrine was the religious expression of the fact that in the commercial world of competition success or fail-ure does not depend upon a man's activity or cleverness, but upon circumstances uncontrollable by him."

An ascent to the atavism of primitive cosmic conceptions, seen through an accidental situation of our day, is always a means of rais-ing a dramatic scene to the heights of tragedy. But our treatment went farther than that. It was pregnant with meaningful sharpnesses along the whole further course of the action.

In Dreiser's book, "for the sake of preserving the honour of the family," Clyde's rich uncle supplies him with the "apparatus" of defence.

The defence lawyers have practically no doubt that Clyde commit-ted a crime. None the less, they invent a "change of heart" he expe-rienced under the influence of his love and pity for Roberta. Simply invented on the spur of the moment, this is pretty good.

But how much greater the irony when there *really* was such a change. When this change was due to quite different motives. When there really was no crime. When the lawyers are convinced that there was a crime. And with a downright lie, so near the truth and at the same time so far from it, they endeavour in this insidious way to whitewash and save the accused.

And the irony becomes still more dramatic and harder to bear when, in the contiguous moment, the "ideology" of your treatment violates the proportions and, in another place, the epic indifference of Dreiser's narrative.

The second volume almost wholly deals with the trial of Clyde for the murder of Roberta and with convicting and sentencing him to the electric chair.

As revealed in a few lines, however, Clyde's conviction is not the true aim of the trial. The sole aim is to boost District Attorney Mason's popularity among the farming population of the state (Roberta was a farmer's daughter), so that they support his nomination as judge.

The defence take on the case, which they knew to be hopeless ("at best ten years in the penitentiary"), for the same political reasons. Belonging to the opposite political camp (but by no means to another class), their primary aim is to exert every effort to defeat the obnoxious prosecutor.

For both sides, Clyde is merely a means to an end.

Already a toy in the hands of "blind Moira—fate," "causality" *à la grecque*, Clyde also becomes a toy in the hands of the far from blind machine of bourgeois justice, machine used as an instrument of political intrigue by extremely sharp-sighted politicians.

Thus the fortunes of the particular case of Clyde Griffiths are tragically expanded and generalized into a real "American tragedy in general"—a characteristic story of a young American at the beginning of the twentieth century.

The whole tangle of design within the trial itself was almost entirely eliminated in the script's construction and was replaced by the pre-election bidding, visible through the traditional solemnity of the courtroom used as nothing more than a drill-ground for a political campaign.

This fundamental treatment of the murder determines the tragic deepening and the strengthened ideological sharpness of yet another part of the film and another figure: Clyde's mother.

She runs a mission. Her religion is a purblind fanaticism. She is so convinced of her absurd dogma that her figure inspires one's involuntary respect and grows almost monumental: one detects the glow of a martyr's aureole.

And that in spite of the fact that she is the first embodiment of the guilt of American society against Clyde: her teachings and principles, her attempt to make him a missionary instead of a worker paved the path to the ensuing tragedy.

Dreiser shows her fighting to the last for her son's innocence, working as a court reporter for a newspaper in order to be near him, touring America (like the mothers and sisters of the Scottsboro boys) with lectures, to collect money to appeal the verdict, when everybody is against him. She definitely acquires the self-sacrificial grandeur of a heroine. In Dreiser's work this grandeur radiates sympathy for her moral and religious doctrines.

In our treatment Clyde, in his death-cell, confesses to his mother that, though he did not kill Roberta, he had planned to do so.

His mother, to whom the word is the deed and the thought of sin equivalent to its execution, is stunned by his confession. And unexpectedly, in a way exactly opposite to the grandeur of the mother in Gorky's novel,* this mother also becomes her son's betrayer. When she goes to the Governor to appeal for her son's life, she is startled by his direct question: "Do you yourself believe in your son's innocence?" At a moment which is to decide the fate of her son—she is silent.

The Christian sophism of an ideal unity (of deed and thought) and a material unity (*de facto*), a parody of dialectics, leads to the final tragic denouement.

The petition is disregarded, and the dogma and dogmatism of its bearer are alike discredited. The mother's fatal moment of silence cannot be washed away by her tears when she takes leave for ever of the son whom she has, with her own hands, delivered into the jaws of the Christian Baal. The sadder these last scenes become, the more bitterly do they lash at the ideology that brought this sadness.

Here, the curious formalism of American dogmatism is supplemented by the seemingly opposite Messianic principle which actually is proved to be the same soulless dogmatism of formal principles in religion. But this is only natural, since both have the same social and class roots.

* Eisenstein means here the character of Mother as presented in the film of N. Zarkhi and V. Pudovkin, because in Gorky's novel there is no betrayal of her son by the mother.—*Ed.*

Eisenstein with students after a conference at the Negro University in New Orleans

Eisenstein in the South of the U.S.A.

In my opinion our treatment succeeded in ripping some of the masks—though not all—from the monumental figure of the mother.

So we "re-formed" the mother and left the Reverend McMillan out of the script.

And Dreiser was the first to salute all that had been brought to his work by our treatment.*

So it is no chance accident that he is drawing away from the petty-bourgeois camp to our own.

In our treatment, the tragedy within the framework of the novel was consummated much earlier than in these final scenes. This end —the cell—the electric chair—the brightly polished spittoon (which I saw myself at Sing-Sing) at his feet—all this is no more than an end to one particular instance of that tragedy which continues to be enacted every hour and every minute in the United States, far *outside the covers of the novel.*

The choice of such a "dry" and "hackneyed" formula of social

---

* S. Eisenstein's archives contain the following letter from T. Dreiser:
    Theodore Dreiser

200 West 57th Street,
New York City,
September 1, 1931.

"Dear Eisenstein:

"I am very much interested by your letter and obliged to you for picturing the difficulties from your point of view. Nothing grieves me more than their refusal to let you make the picture. I was satisfied Paramount had no one who could do it as well as you could have done it, and the absolutely practical and material way in which they side-tracked this original plan infuriated me.

"As you saw, I did my best to prevent production, but the decision enclosed will make clear to you what happened. Also the judicial attitude in regard to the moving picture in America as such. We now have a legal interpretation of what its approach should be!

"What are you doing in Mexico? Are you making a film, and if so, what kind of a film are you making, and how are you managing to live and be comfortable down there?

"Have you any idea that *An American Tragedy* could ever be filmed in Russia? I wish it might be. At any rate, I want you to know that I hold you and your very distinguished work in the greatest admiration, and that I hope the time will come when there may be something of mine that will fall not only into your hands but your power to produce.

"Did you ever read my tragedy entitled *The Hand of the Potter*? If not, I should like to send you a copy.

"My best wishes as always."

treatment affords more than a sharpening of situations and a deepening revelation of images and characters.

... It was Josef von Sternberg who actually made the film which proved to the the exact opposite of what we had planned. He literally discarded everything on which our treatment had been based and restored everything that we had discarded.

As for an "inner monologue," it did not occur to him.

Sternberg confined his attention to the "front office's" wishes and filmed a straight detective case.

The old grey lion Dreiser battled for our "distortion" of his work, and sued Paramount, who had filmed a formally and outwardly correct version of his story.

1932

A FEW THOUGHTS ABOUT SOVIET COMEDY

This happened in Paris, early in the spring of 1930. But it was not the friendly Paris with which our country is working for a peaceful world policy. It was the post-Kutepov* Paris, when rupture of diplomatic relations between the two countries was expected every day.

The atmosphere was tense. And it was in such an atmosphere that I was to make a report at the Sorbonne, or, to be more exact, to say a few words before the demonstration of *The General Line* (*Old and New*).

Half an hour before the beginning the police banned the showing of the film, but the auditorium was full and something simply had to be done. The only thing left was to stretch out my introductory remarks into a regular report, and, since that would not be enough for the whole evening either, start a "Questions and Answers" game with the audience.

A dangerous and exciting game, that, and all the more so when there are persons bent on "catching" you with all kinds of insinuat-

---

* In 1930, Kutepov, a tsarist general and deadly enemy of the Soviet Union, was kidnapped in Paris by White Guards who raised a hue and cry that the crime was "perpetrated by the Bolsheviks" and thus tried to whip up anti-Soviet sentiments in France.—*Ed.*

Eisenstein during the shooting of *Old and New (The General Line)* (courtesy The Museum of Modern Art/Film Stills Archive)

Shooting *Old and New:* peasant-actors holding reflector; Eisenstein; Eduard Tisse behind camera (courtesy The Museum of Modern Art/Film Stills Archive)

Shooting *Old and New:* Eisenstein, left (courtesy The Museum of Modern Art/Film Stills Archive)

Shooting *Old and New:* Eduard Tisse with camera on trac-
tor; Eisenstein in cap on extreme right (courtesy The Museum of Modern Art/Film Stills Archive)

ing, hostile, tricky and equivocal questions. Later I learned that police pickets were stationed outside the Sorbonne; lorries full of plain-clothes men waited near by. M.Chiappe* himself was rushing to and fro, anticipating a skirmish and hoping to take advantage of the turmoil to detain undesirable persons: after all, the audience included representatives of the "other side" too, including Marcel Cachin.

The game went on successfully for more than an hour. The questions and answers came with lightning rapidity. The audience was in a responsive mood. We were never at a loss for a repartee. But it was time to finish. I was anxiously watching for a question that would enable me to close the debate with a flourish.

At last it came.

A lean, malicious-looking, sallow-faced individual rose in the gallery.

"Why aren't there any comedies in your country? Is it true the Soviets have killed laughter?"

A deadly silence ensued.

Usually I am slow at finding a proper answer, especially in front of the public. But this time I had a brain-wave. Instead of replying, I burst out laughing.

"They'll roar with laughter in the Soviet Union when I tell them of your question!"

We concluded the meeting amid general merriment and left the building by way of the old Sorbonne yard. The university looked like a besieged fortress. But nothing untoward occurred.

We had conducted the debate in a seemingly free and easy manner and finished it with laughter.

There were no objective grounds for police interference. No one can be arrested for laughing.

The next morning some of the newspapers wrote: "Bolsheviks with daggers in their teeth are not so dangerous as Bolsheviks with a smile on their lips."

But I read no papers that day: I spent it at police-stations, gendarmerie, the Prefecture. They ordered me to leave Paris, France. But that is beside the point. What I am concerned with in this article is

* Paris police commissioner.—*Tr.*

laughter. I ask myself, Do we laugh? Yes. Then what must our laughter be like?

What must our laughter be like, and especially what kind of laughter will the screen evoke? This question has been asked repeatedly and many have tried to answer it. Some answers have been too simple. Others, too complicated.

A few years ago I worked on the script of a comedy.

I have a strictly academical approach to all I do. I make use of all available scientific data; I discuss with myself problems of programme and principle; I make calculations and draw inferences. I "dissect music" in the course of its progress, and sometimes anticipating its progress, with the result that its elements are buried in my drawers among heaps of material relating to principle. I stop writing the scenario and instead plunge into research work, filling pages and pages with it. I don't know which is more useful but abandoning creative work for scientific analysis is what I am often guilty of. Very often I settle a particular problem of principle only to lose all interest in its practical application.

That is exactly what happened to my comedy. All I have been able to analyze and determine will go into a book and not on the screen.

Perhaps I should never have produced a Soviet film comedy. One thing, however, is quite clear: I adhere to the tradition of laughing while the lash swishes. Mine is the laughter of destruction.

The lash has already swished in the attempts at comedy made here and there in *Old and New.* The swishing is heard still more distinctly in the comedy I have left unfinished.

But I have not wasted the time I spent on it: I have proved to myself one point of principle.

What is Chaplin remarkable for? What makes him tower over all other film comedians?

His profound lyricism. His ability to make his spectators shed genuine tears. Chaplin is a lovable crank. A grown-up behaving like a child.

Then an idea came to me: Chaplin and the future of our comedy.

The simplest way (that is, plain plagiarism) would be to dress up characters suitably, think up new situations and preserve Chaplin's important contribution to the film art. This could be called an experiment—just to avoid censure.

But we could not do that, of course.

I think that logic and inspiration have enabled me to discover something equivalent to Chaplin's contribution which will enrich the *genre* of our film comedy.

In my opinion, it is not the lyrical and the sentimental (in the positive sense of the term) that will be the distinctive feature of our high screen genre. No, it will be something else.

While in Chaplin's films we have love of mankind, solicitude for the "smaller brother," tears for the humiliated and insulted, for those whom fate maltreats, in our films we will have social emotion—socialist love of mankind. And socialist love of mankind is not compassion but re-creation; comedy scenes are socially, not individually, lyrical. But social lyricism is pathos. The lyricism of the masses is a hymn. A comedy evoking not lyrical but pathetic tears—this is how I visualized the comedy in our film art.

The second point is that it will have not only a generalized type like Chaplin. It will have types which at the same time will be notions. (Can you imagine—a notion sitting down or having a shave, taking off its hat or going to bed!)

We all start our lives as exploiters. For nine months we draw our life's sustenance from our mothers. For many more months we nurse at their breasts.

In our biological development childhood is the period of exploitation and consumption. While this period lasts it is timely and even pleasant. But if it lasts beyond its natural time it is disgusting and fit only for idiots.

Social relations of exploitation were conducive to progress at certain stages of social development. In its initial phase the bourgeoisie was a progressive class. But relations of exploitation mean social infancy. The disgusting nature of these relations becomes apparent as soon as humanity has learned to use its feet. Actually, as soon as they appear.

The object of our ridicule will be this trait—social infancy crawling over into the age of social maturity, I should say, socialist maturity.

One cannot help laughing while watching Chaplin, playing a paper hanger, manicure his nails with huge wall-paper scissors. But this stunt is individual and illogical.

The nature of laughter is different, and the terms "ours" and "alien," though hackneyed, preserve their significance. One and the same action may convey widely different meanings.

Now let us take, not idiotism, but lyricism, sentiment and feeling.

The finale of *The Pilgrim* is one of the best scenes in Chaplin comedies.

Chaplin, an escaped convict, disguises as a minister. His masquerade proves fatal, for the parishioners get hold of him and he is compelled to preach. And he does, giving a brilliant performance of David's combat with Goliath. (This is one of the funniest scenes in Chaplin's repertoire). Then the church money is stolen. Chaplin's identity becomes known. But he did not take the money: on the contrary, he found the money and returned it. The right of property has not been violated. But Chaplin *is* a convict. The law, too, must be inviolate. And we see the wretched little prisoner tramping along a dusty road, escorted by a mounted sheriff. The sheriff, at heart, is like Javert, the detective in Hugo's *Les misérables*. When Javert becomes convinced of the goodness of Jean Valjean, the former convict he has persecuted half his life, he fails to do his duty for the first time in his life: he leaves his post, so to speak, and lets Valjean go. Valjean is free.

The sheriff is sentimental. He wants to let the "good" convict go. And here is Chaplin's masterpiece: the sheriff is escorting him along the Mexican border. But it does not enter the highly-principled convict's head to escape across the border to free Mexico. He does not get the sheriff's hints. Then comes the best moment of all: the sheriff asks his prisoner ... to pick a flower for him, on the other side of the border, in Mexico. Chaplin obligingly crosses the border. The sheriff, the load off his mind, gives the spurs to his horse. But ... Chaplin catches up with him and gives him the flower.

As far as I remember, Chaplin gets kicked in the pants and the concluding shots show him walking away, one foot in the U.S.A. and the other in Mexico, the border lying between his feet. No solution.

We know how the Bolsheviks fight.

We know how the Bolsheviks work.

We know how the Bolsheviks gain their victories.

And today we see how the Bolsheviks laugh.

"Our laughter" and "their laughter" are no abstractions: they are divided by an abyss of social significance.

What, then, will be the comedy and laughter brought to the world by the young proletarian class which took power in October and, holding it firmly in its strong hands, is advancing to final victory?

Will this laughter be the result of idle fun and merrymaking after a good meal or an attempt to escape from life's adversities? Will it be mild irony at the humorous misfortunes of a lovable crank?

No. Laughter in Russia is traditionally different. It is bound with the works of such immortal writers as Gogol, Chekhov and Saltykov-Shchedrin, and its characteristic feature has always been social exposure.

From the mild irony of Chekhov, through the bitterness of Gogol's "laughter through tears," to the swishing lash of Shchedrin's pamphlets and satire.

What will be the laughter which is to take the place of that of Chekhov, Gogol and Shchedrin?

Will it follow the line of carefree American guffaws or preserve the tradition of the bitter laughter of Russia's nineteenth-century comics?

All of us will have to be present at the birth of the new type of laughter, nay, take an active part in writing a new page in the world history of humour and laughter, just as the Soviet Union has written a new page in the history of social structures.

The time has not yet come for us to indulge in carefree laughter: socialism has not yet been built. So there is no call for light-heartedness.

Laughter is a new kind of weapon. A type of light gun, very effective in cases where there is no need to employ heavy tanks of social wrath.

Pamphlet, satire, laughter in the stifling atmosphere of nineteenth-century tsarist Russia and everywhere in the twentieth century, with the exception of Russia which has become the U.S.S.R., have served as vehicles of protest. In our country the task of laughter is to kill off the enemy, just as it is the task of infantry to flood enemy trenches after heavy artillery has cleared the way for the sharp bayonet. There, laughter announces the beginning of battle; here it heralds our victory.

That is what I think of the nature and role of laughter in the conditions of the last encounters with the class enemy, who uses every imaginable (and unimaginable) opportunity to stop the triumphant march of socialism.

A comedy personage, a comedy type in Western Europe and America is a funny representative of its social environment; the ridicule often does not go beyond the positions of chauvinism or nationalism. At least this is true of the cinema from which all vestiges of militant class humour are being thrown out.

We can rise above the limits of purely biological laughter only if we rise to the level of understanding the social significance of the wry face which we make the target of our ridicule.

The comic quality of a social mask and the devastating force of social ridicule must and will form the basis of militant humour, the inevitable form of our laughter.

It seems to me that that is what laughter will be at the stage of the last and decisive battles for the triumph of socialism in one country.

1937

WOLVES AND SHEEP

(Directors and Actors)

As a matter of principle, I am all for the collective method of work and consider suppression of the initiative of any member of a collective body absolutely wrong. Moreover, I expressed this idea very emphatically at the U.S.S.R. Conference of Cinema Workers: "Only a talentless collective can exist when one creative personality tries to dominate another."

And yet in this problem, too, the struggle goes on two fronts and there are cases when a director's "iron heel" is not only justified but absolutely necessary.

No one will dispute the fact that unity of style, both in visualizing and producing a film, is an indispensable condition for creative director-actor cooperation. The importance of this condition is all the greater if a film is to be stylistically *distingué* (not stylized!).

Unity makes any form of creative cooperation possible—not only between a director and an actor, but between a director and a composer and, particularly, between a cameraman and a director. This applies primarily to the cinema, where all these problems acquire particular significance and acuteness. Cooperation exists in every collective where there is unity of style.

When, then, is a "conflict" justified? When can the director behave like a "tyrant"? First, when a member of the collective does not fully perceive the importance of stylistic requirements. For, dictatorship, etc., apart, it is the director who is responsible for the organic unity of style of the film. That is his function and in this sense he is a unifier. Stylistic unity can and should be achieved by the whole collective, and in this respect the legitimate theatre has an advantage in that the participants work together and mature as they rehearse a play. Individuals merge with the whole conception of the play.

Work on motion pictures is much more difficult. Here, once an action is fixed on celluloid, it remains there; with visions being strictly numbered in a script, without the "revelations" of a dress rehearsal, work is more complicated and the actor's participation and appearance in the film are restricted to a greater degree. Perhaps the most difficult thing here for an actor is to harmonize his own solution with the style of the specifically cinema elements, and it is not always that he understands and grasps them all. The compositional line of, say, shots and montage should obviously be in the same key with the rest of the elements, and the various modes of music, shades in the characterization, structure of shots, and montage constructions are not always in keeping with one another. Hence, none of the elements which are combined creatively is free; none of them can fall out of the key, or bedlam will be the result. And then take the specific nature of work in the motion pictures. For instance, unlike a stage actor whose creative participation in, or at least presence at, all the phases of the rehearsal is not only desirable but obligatory, a screen player cannot visualize the entire shooting process of a picture.

A cinema actor must, therefore, be endowed with extra-sharp intuition as regards the style and the key of the film as a whole. The actor's own treatment, stylistically foreign to the whole, must interfere with the general conception as little as possible. For the general conception provides one style and one key to the compositional whole, to the plastic form of all the shots (including the angle from which a rye field or night lighting is shot), and a *note* of foreign intonation, a different rhythm of action, while not contradicting the general conception of a role, may prove absolutely foreign to the film and actually seem borrowed from another picture.

An actor's sensitivity, strengthened by a director's explanations and demonstrations, their stylistic colouring, suggests to the actor the aspect in which all the other elements are solved. The tonality that distinguishes Shishkin's popular painting of a she-bear and her cubs will be completely out of place in a construction in the style of Serov. The same applies to orchestration: a composer will not use a wrong timbre. And a realistic folk melody will not necessarily be treated naturalistically, that is, played on a folk instrument.

This is where the attacks on the dictatorial methods of some directors spring from. But these directors aim at the best solution—they do not want to confine their art to mere representative verisimilitude but strive for a stylistically imagist unity of composition. For this a very sensitive ear is needed. But there are some with no ear at all and in such cases the director must step in and offer his corrections. This wounds the *amour-propre* of those whose style is being corrected. And the result is that the director is denounced as a dictator.

That is where I see the roots of the director-actor problem.

1935

NOT COLOURED, BUT IN COLOUR

Sound did not take root in the film as a whim, novelty, or freak.

Strictly speaking, it did not take root in the silent film but sprang from it.

Sound sprang from the inner urge present in the silent film to go beyond the limits of plastic expressiveness alone.

This urge to give play to its potentialities was present in the silent film since its inception.

From its very first steps our silent film strove by all attainable means to convey not only the plastic but also the sound image.

Attempts in this direction were made as early as in *Strike*,* which contained a short scene that proved very popular, showing the strikers discussing their plans under the pretext of holding a picnic with an accordion.

The scene ended with a sequence in which we tried to convey the idea of sound by purely visual means. The functions of the two strips of the future—the representations and the sound track—were here performed by a double exposure. In the first was the white blotch of the pond at the foot of the hill, losing itself in the distance. From the pond in the background, groups of merry-makers were moving upwards, towards the camera. The second, serving as a rhythmic border to the landscape, was a close-up of moving gleaming stripes—the lighted ribs of the accordion bellows. The movements, shown from different angles, were superimposed on the first and created the illusion of a moving melody accompanying the scene. This was a kind of a silent "forefather" of the "cinema accordion" which is apt to set our teeth on edge in sound films.

*October*** was full of sounds expressed by means of plastic constructions.

In its variety of such constructions the film could be said to rival Bryusov's collection of poetic "experiments." There is hardly a complex form of verse, rarely used or never used at all, that Bryusov did not experiment with, either out of curiosity or a desire to polish up his virtuosity.

Encroachments on the sphere of sound in the silent film *October* were equally numerous. In some places we succeeded in conveying the din made by machine-guns as they were being dragged into the Smolny. The suggestion of sound was furnished by the disproportionately large size of the machine-gun wheels, achieved by filming the corridor and the machine-guns rolling in the foreground from a very low camera set-up.

This suggestion of sound was completed by the frightened faces of Mensheviks popping out of doors marked "private" as the machine-guns rumbled by in the corridor.

---

* Eisenstein's first film, made in 1924, released in 1925.—*Ed.*
** A film made by Eisenstein together with G. V. Alexandrov in 1927 to mark the tenth anniversary of the October Revolution.—*Ed.*

In other cases this was done by means of a system of alternating and slow-motion iris diaphragms opening and shutting the palace halls. This was to convey the idea of the echo of the *Aurora*'s salvo reverberating in the Winter Palace.

Sometimes the audience was shown a rapid succession of shots with the crystal chandeliers twinkling in the light. The impression was that the crystals were jingling in response to the gunfire.

Finally, we went to the length of unashamedly presenting close-ups of harps or balalaikas to ridicule the conciliatory tongue-wagging of the October Revolution's opponents at the Second Congress of Soviets. In such cases the montage was ponderous and baroque in form: what would have been easy for the sound track required an enormous effort to achieve by plastic means.

Thus, the urge for sound was evident in silent films many years before the sound problem was technically solved: the silent cinema yearned for sound, for the effect of sound, for the sound image, and for sound associations.

The urge for colour in the film is equally strong.

As the silent film cried out for sound, so does the sound film cry out for colour.

I shall say later why the urge for colour is especially poignant in the sound film. Here I intend to discuss why colour in itself is a natural feature of the cinema.

The best works of our cameramen have long been potentially in colour in their essence. True, the scale of colours is limited to white, grey and black, but the paucity of the expressive means has never been felt in the best films and they have never been regarded as "tricolour."

Their composition is so colour-saturated that such great artists as Tisse, Moskvin and Kosmatov seem to have deliberately confined themselves to the white, grey and black, although they might use the entire spectrum.

Just as in a passage of his overture to *Iolanthe* Chaikovsky confined himself to one colour only—the wind instruments.

Just as in Act II of the ballet *Romeo and Juliet* Prokofiev confines himself to mandolins, although he could have used the whole orchestra.

The black, grey and white hues in the films of our best cameramen were never regarded as colourless, but as possessing a colour which (or the variations of which) prevailed not only in the pl unity of the film's colouring but in the thematic unity and the m ment of the film as a whole.

Grey was the dominant colour in *Potemkin*. It was made up of three basic elements: the hard steely gleam of the battleship's boards; the mellow tonality of grey mists *à la* Whistler; and a third element which can be said to synthesize the first two, combining the gleam of the first and the mellowness of the second—a variation of the sea surface photographed in the grey gamut.

The grey in the film was brought to its extremes. It was brought to black—the black coats of the officers and the black shots of the night of anxiety. And it was brought to white—the white tarpaulin in the shooting scene, the white sails of the yawls speeding towards the *Potemkin*; the white sailors' caps flying up in the final scene, the explosion-like burst of the tarpaulin shroud torn by the pressure of the revolutionary year 1905.

October was filmed in velvety-black tones. With a black gleam like that seen in real life on rain-wetted monuments and roads and in photographs on gold, gilded and bronze things.

In *Old and New* the dominant tone was white. The white state farm. White milk. Flowers. White struggled through the grey beginning, symbolizing poverty. It struggled through the black of crime and felony.

White, the colour of joy and symbol of new forms of management, became more and more pronounced. White appeared at the climactic point of the film—in the cream separator sequence with everybody anxiously waiting for the first white drop of milk. Appearing on the screen together with that first drop, white brought joy to it in the shots showing the state farm, the streams of milk, the herds of animals and flocks of birds.

The red of the flag pierced *Potemkin* like a fanfare but here its effect was due not so much to the colour itself as to its meaning.

So when we approach the problem of colour in film we must think first of all of the meaning associated with a given colour. Golovnya's *Mother* shows similar play of colour though less pronouncedly than Tisse's films: it begins with the oily black of greased boots and through the darkness of the night search with its Rembrandt-like lighting, through the greyness of the prison it reaches the whiteness of the floating ice stressed by dark masses of people with lit-up faces.

Preserving in *Alexander Nevsky* all the achievements of the silent film in the sphere of colour associations (and surprising the critics and press abroad by showing the villains in sparkling white and not in traditional black), Tisse went still farther in this respect.

Devil alone knows how and by what technical means, but he managed to create an unmistakable illusion of colour.

In the Battle on the Ice sequence the sky sometimes looks blue to me and the grass greyish-green at the beginning. Likewise the shots of Bozhenko's funeral in *Shchors* seem golden passing into indigo and the opening sequence of [Dovzhenko's] *Ivan* bluish-green.

With the advent of sound these "colour elements" of formally non-colour photography took on a new meaning. For it is thanks to these elements of photography that sound and picture are blended most completely and harmoniously. If the image remains the decisive factor of the audio-visual combination, as we wrote long ago in our *Statement* on the sound film; if movement opens with the rhythmic and the texture of the material filmed with the timbre blending of the visual and auditory elements; then its harmonious blending with sound is probably attained best through light nuances, inseparable from colour nuances.

And we can definitely state that complete organic unity—the unity of picture and sound—will be achieved only when we have films in colour. Only then will we be able to find the subtlest visual equivalent to the subtlest curve in melody. Only then complete visual orchestration will rise to the level of the wealth of orchestration in music.

Only then will it be possible to overtake and surpass the visions of Diderot, Wagner and Scriabin who dreamed of an audio-visual synthesis.

I advisedly say *in colour* and not *coloured*, to preclude any association with something coloured, painted.

We must not allow the plastic austerity of the screen to turn all of a sudden into a piece of gay printed calico or gaudily painted postcard. We do not want to see such postcards on the screen. We want this new screen to show us colours in organic unity with the

Scene from *Alexander Nevsky* with villains dressed in white (courtesy The Museum of Modern Art/Film Stills Archive)

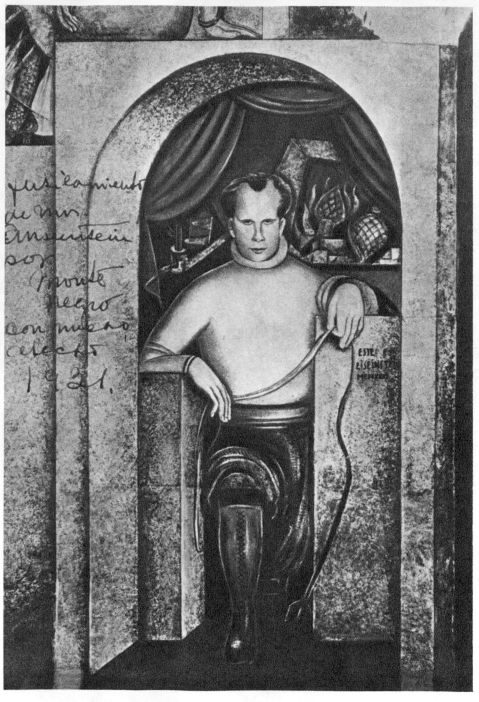

A fresco by R. Montenegro at the Colegio de Pedro y
Pablo in Mexico. The legend reads "This is Eisenstein"

image and the theme, the content and the drama, the actio
the music. Together with these, colour will be a new potent
of film impressiveness and film idiom.

May the achievements of our expert cameramen, of which I spoke
above, serve to accomplish a threefold aim:

May they give us courage, daring and audacity.

For they remind us of the fact that a true organic sense of colour
has long pervaded our films, that it has been developing along with
our cinema itself, that we have many artists who have a true feeling
for the colour element and a knowledge of how to use it, and that

the tasks of colour in the film are *not* what we see in technically
perfect American films.

All this inspires us with confidence that our cinema, permeated as
it is with the loftiest ideas and greatest passions of our times, will
be able to make a decisive contribution to the sphere of colour film.
1940

COLOUR FILM*

Dear Lev Vladimirovich,

You asked me to write a few words about colour in the films for
the second edition of your book, quite correctly assuming that without some practical experience, all speculations about colour composition will invariably prove abstractions or groundless fancies.

I gladly comply with your request, writing on the basis of the experience I gained working on a colour sequence in *Ivan the Terrible.*

There is a viewpoint on the use of expressive means in cinematography which, in my opinion, is erroneous but which, nevertheless, is fairly widespread.

This viewpoint holds that good music in a film is that which you
do not hear; that good camera work is that which is unobtrusive;
and that good direction is that which you do not notice. As regards
colour, this viewpoint holds that in a good colour film you are not
conscious of colour. To my mind, this viewpoint, raised to the
level of a principle, is a reflection of creative impotence, of inability to master the complex of cinematic expressive means needed to
make an organic film.

* This article was written as a letter to film director L. Kuleshov.—*Ed.*

It is noteworthy that this viewpoint is advocated by directors whose abilities are limited to handling actors, but who are helpless when it comes to working with the cameraman, the composer, the designer, etc., on the music score, shots, landscape, editing, colour, and in all other spheres of film production.

In my opinion, the great variety of expressive means in the films should by no means allow film-makers to neglect one for the sake of another.

On the contrary, they should be able to make full use of the potentialities of each and to assign to it the proper place it deserves in the general *ensemble* of the film.

I have deliberately used the term *"ensemble,"* for, just as the *ensemble* of actors relies on each being given a chance to express himself to the best of his abilities and on a skilful balance of these individual expressions through proper **"orchestration,"** so must the entire complex of the expressive means of the film be so used as to make each of them effective to the utmost within the framework of the whole.

The word "orchestration," too, has been used deliberately, because the orchestra will always be the example of the harmony one must strive for. We do not hear deafening *tutti* all the time; the orchestra treats us to a most wisely coordinated interaction and interchange of the means of musical expressiveness through individual parts, which does not prevent the leading ones from preserving their place and allows each individual instrument to show itself at its best in its proper place and in conformity with the theme.

Similarly, the expressive whole of a work of film art must be based not on the suppression of certain elements and their "neutralization" in favour of others, but on a wise employment of those expressive means which can, at the given moment, give the fullest scope to that element which, under given conditions, is capable of revealing with utmost clarity the content, meaning, theme and idea of the film.

Is it not obvious that in filming, say, the burning of Moscow, the producer must be able to present the passions burning in the breasts of his characters, the fire of their patriotism as convincingly as the flames raging in our ancient capital? Is it not equally obvious that a failure to present this "elemental" part of the film expressively as a whole will affect, first of all, that emotional power of experiencing and acting which is the most important element in the unfolding of the theme? This element, however, is effective only when it is backed by the combined power of the other components, the rest of the expressive means participating in the general "chorus" to the best of their abilities and in conformity with the composition of the whole..

I repeat that mastery here means ability to develop each element of the expressive means to the utmost, at the same time orchestrating, balancing the whole so as to prevent any particular, individual element from undermining the unity of the *ensemble*, the unity of the compositional whole.

This idea is in direct opposition to the pessimistic stand on the expressive means advocated by creatively weak personalities, who disguise their impotence by the desirability to keep film components "unnoticeable" and masquerade their inability to manage them by a desire to "neutralize" expressive elements.

Such is the position one should take in regard to any expressive means of film-making.

It applies in similar measure to colour.

The meaning of all I have said above may be reduced to the following: all elements of cinematic expressiveness must participate in the making of a film as elements of dramatic action.

Hence, the first condition for the use of colour in a film is that it must be, first and foremost, a dramatic factor.

In this respect colour is like music.

Music in films is good when it is necessary.

Colour, too, is good when it is necessary.

That means that colour and music are both good where and when they (*they* and not the other elements) can most fully express or explain what must be conveyed, said, or elucidated at the given moment of the development of action.

This may be a monologue ("A million tortures"—Chatsky in *Wit Works Woe*), an exclamation ("*Et tu, Brute!*") or a pause ("The people keep silence"—*Boris Godunov*).

This may be the movement of a mass of objects ("Birnam wood coming to Dunsinane"—*Macbeth*), a hardly perceptible gesture ("With a slight wave of his hand he sent his troops against the

Russians"—*Poltava*), sometimes the movement of the orchestra using the fateful theme to make way for itself among the arias (*The Queen of Spades*), sometimes sunrise flooding the stage with blood-red light heralding the hero's death (*Ivan Susanin*). In its own place, at a given moment, each is the protagonist for the moment, occupying the leading place in the general chorus of expressive elements which yield it this place—for the moment.

Silence. A word. A tirade.

Mass evolutions. A slight wave of the hand.

Aria or an orchestra passage.

The colour element invading the stage.

Each in its own place. Each as the vehicle for a certain dramaturgically unique moment. Each as the most perfect expressive element of the general idea at the moment it unfolds. The impact of the expressive means proceeds in chords.

Sometimes the pronounced word is appropriately supported by music coming from a distance, as, for instance, a dirge sung under the vaults, a shepherd's pipe in the mist-enveloped field, a waltz played in the room next door. At others music is not appropriate, but the inner urge for it is such that the impossibility to account for its source in an everyday way cannot serve as an obstacle to its use.

Sometimes the raging elements pounce upon the audience together with a chaos of sounds, or a slowly floating moon introduces a transparent "blue" lyrical theme into the soft music.

Any of these methods can be used, for music lends to acting or a situation, a scene or a pause in development that irresistible power of emotional impact which, out of all the means of dramaturgic expressiveness, is at that particular time the most effective in giving vent to the dramaturgic moment, the link in the chain of the dramaturgic whole.

At each given moment each element must remain within its strictly defined bounds. Knowing it is to blossom forth in a few minutes as the leading element, it should disguise itself for the time being, appear dull, let others drown out its sound, be as inconspicuous as possible.

But this self-effacement is not "neutralization." It is a retreat before a better leap is made. The deliberate inconspicuousness is to enhance the effect of the emergence of the element in question.

We regard colour as an element of the film's dramaturgy.

The application of colour seems to be similar to that of music.

The argument that in a colour film colour is present on the screen all the time whereas music is introduced only when it is necessary, does not change the matter. Because we do not call a film a musical in which at one moment we see an accordion-player and at another hear a ditty sung, while the rest is taken up by dialogue.

A film is a musical if the absence of music is regarded as a pause or *caesura* (it may last a whole reel, but it must be as precise as the rhythmically calculated measures of silence on the sound track). In such a case musical continuity is not broken: when no music is heard from the screen there is a *musical dialogue* (and not merely carelessly thrown lines), a plastic succession of landscape elements, a throbbing tissue of emotions portrayed by the characters, a montage rhythm within the episodes and the sequence of the episodes.

The same applies to colour.

So long as the situation does not require the colour element to give a dramaturgic expression to action and no bright blue or gold diverts our attention from the whispered words; so long as it does not flood the screen with the gaudy green of the heroine's dress as we drink in the words falling from the quivering lips on her deathly pale face, colour veils its self-asserting power and acts as a frame which, in the interests of the close-up, excludes all that is not essential, all that, given in a long shot, might draw our attention away from the object presented in the close-up.

But this, too, is not "neutralization." It is a "colour pause," accumulation by the colour element of force in order to overwhelm the spectator with the bluish-black indigo of waves edged by white foam, or with torrents of fiery-red lava out of dark brown clouds of smoke precisely at a moment when neither acting nor mass movements nor the image of the great element itself, even supported by blaring helicons, can be relied upon to impress fully and completely without colour.

But enough of piling one "picturesque" word upon another in emotionally coloured descriptions.

Let us pass over to the prose of colour craftsmanship in filmmaking.

Having established that the "colour line" weaves its way through the plot as one more independent part in the dramaturgic counter-point of the film's expressive means, let us study in detail "how it is done" and "what it requires," how a "colour image" differs from "coloured objects of representation" and "coloured pictures" of individual shots substituting for a through-going colour suite which embodies the meaningful "colour dramaturgic line" of the whole.

There are two aspects to the dramatic function of colour: subor-dination of the colour element to a definite dramaturgic structure (which determines the structure of the film through all the ele-ments, including colour) and broader understanding of colour through the dramatic presentation of the active element within it (which gives expression to the conscious and volitional impulse in the one who uses it, as distinct from the indefinite *status quo* of a given colour in nature).

There is a difference between the process of the development of colour expressiveness and the status of colour in nature and in phenomena where it exists despite the will of the one who creates "something that never existed" from "something that exists," some-thing that serves to express the ideas and feelings of the creator.

As soon as we approach colour from this standpoint we recog-nize a familiar situation. We see that the problem facing us as we strive to master colour creatively is very much like the one we en-countered when we had to master montage, and later, audio-visual combinations and, we may presume, like the problem which will arise when we pass to stereoscopic films and television.

What essentially was the significance of passing from photo-graphy "from one angle" to "montage photography"?

I wrote about this a long time ago and practised it still earlier, always proceeding from only one principle—destruction of the in-definite and neutral, existing "in itself," no matter whether it be an event or a phenomenon, and its reassembly in accordance with the idea dictated by attitude to this event or phenomenon, an atti-tude which, in its turn, is determined by my ideology, my outlook, that is to say, *our* ideology, *our* outlook.

It is at that moment that passive representation gives way to conscious reflection of phenomena of life, history, nature, events, actions, and human behaviour. It is at that moment that a living dynamic image takes place of passive reproduction.

The latter is symbolized, as it were, by a "long shot" where the interrelations of the elements are predetermined by their existence and not relations, where the order of presentation does not depend on the will of the presenter, where no emphasis is laid on the decisive factor, where the secondary is mixed up with the main, where the interconnection between the elements of a phenomenon does not express connection as I understand it, and so on and so forth.

(I do not mean a well-constructed "long shot" built up on the compositional principle of a picture that is remarkable for being a whole in the strict sense of montage, but a piece of an event "as it exists" caught by the camera at random.)

In the development of the montage method the "long shot" was broken up into separate elements. These elements were endowed with importance of varying degrees through the increase or decrease of their size, and new continuity and connection were established between them. All this was done with the sole purpose of imbuing what was hitherto a passive phenomenon with dynamic and dramatic action, revealing the maker's attitude to the phenomenon, his appraisal of it as a manifestation of his outlook.

We see that a consciously creative approach to the phenomenon presented begins at the moment when the unrelated coexistence of phenomena is disjoined and replaced by the casual interconnection of its elements dictated by the film-maker's attitude to the phenomenon, which, in its turn, is determined by his outlook.

It is at this moment that the montage method becomes a means of film expressiveness.

The same thing occurs in the case of audio-visual montage.

The art of audio-visual montage begins at the moment when, after a period of simply reflecting obvious connections, the film-maker starts to establish them himself,.selecting such connections as reflect the essence of the content it is his aim to portray and to impress upon the spectator.

Strictly speaking, the audio-visual film became a special means of expressiveness in art at the moment when the creaking of a boot was separated from the representation of the boot itself and combined with a ... human face, anxiously listening to the sound. Here the process we discussed earlier stands out with still greater clarity.

First, we sever the passive everyday connection between an object and the sound it makes. Second, we establish a new connection which is in keeping with the theme I deem necessary to discuss and not with the customary "order of things."

What I am interested in at present is not the fact that a boot usually creaks. What I am interested in is the reaction of my hero, or villain, or any other character; I am interested in the connection with another event, which I myself establish in order to express my theme most fully at a given moment.

This is quite obvious in regard to audio-visual combinations, for here we have the two spheres we must combine in the shape of two strips of film, one bearing the representations, the other the sound track.

The various combinations of the two strips with each other and with numberless other sound tracks, serve only further to complicate and enrich that stream of audio-visual images which link up to express my theme; they undermine the stagnant "order of things" for the sake of expressing *my*, the author's, attitude to this "order of things."

We must bear all this in mind when we approach colour, and I dwell so persistently on the preceding stages precisely because without thoroughly grasping this process in its application to colour, the purposeful "development of the colour element" throughout the film is impossible, just as it is impossible without it to establish the most elementary principles of the "development of the colour element" in the cinema.

It's no use tackling colour-film production unless we feel that the "line" of colour movement through the film progresses as independently as the "line" of music which passes through the entire film. It was all very graphically shown in the case of representations and sound track, which can be easily joined together to produce any audio-visual combinations.

It may be seen still more clearly in the combination of several "lines"—parts of the different instruments in the orchestra, or in superimposing sound tracks (the simplest case—the "line" of the dialogue superimposed on the "line" of music and the sound-effects "line" superimposed on the two).

But the "colour line" is much more difficult to feel and to follow through the "line" of object representations although it permeates the latter as does the "line" of music.

And yet, without this feeling and the system of concrete methods of solving colour problems born of this feeling, no practical work with colour is possible.

The film-maker must psychologically grasp the method of "separation" which was used in the initial stages of mastering montage constructions and audio-visual combinations, for this method is absolutely essential for mastery and artistry in both spheres.

What must be "separated" in the present instance are the colouring of an object and its "colour sound," which form an inseparable whole in our notion of colour.

Just as the creaking of a boot had to be separated from the boot before it became an element of expressiveness, so must the notion of "orange colour" be separated from the colouring of an orange, before colour becomes part of a system of consciously controlled means of expression and impression. Before we can learn to distinguish three oranges on a patch of lawn both as three objects in the grass *and* as three orange patches against a green background, we dare not think of colour composition.

Because, unless we develop that ability, we cannot establish the colour-compositional connection between these oranges and two orange-coloured buoys floating on the surface of limpid greenish-blue water.

We cannot follow the *crescendo* presented by the movement, from piece to piece, from pure orange to reddish orange, and the greenness of the grass, through the bluish green of the water, to the orange-red patches of the buoys glowing like red poppies against the sky preserving a tint of the greenness but recently seen as the dominant note in the waves of a bay, to which we had been led by the scarcely-perceptible blue hues in the lush green grass.

For the orange does not become a poppy by going through a buoy.

And grass does not become sky by going through water.

But the orange colour, going through reddish orange, finds its consummation in red, and azure is born from bluish green engendered by pure green with a spark of blue in it.

For some reason or other we feel the need of a series of objects: the three oranges, the two buoys and the poppies are blended by one common movement of colour supported by the tints of the background. This is exactly what used to happen in former days when as a framework for such unity we utilized (in static sequences) the outlines and tonal "sounds" of grey photography, capable of producing a unified visual whole out of the pattern of a woman's shawl, the contours of tree branches and the fleecy clouds above; or (in dynamic sequences) a correctly calculated increase in the tempo from shot to shot.

That is what happens on a purely plastic plane, on a plastic plane unrelated to other elements.

The same happens when colour movement ceases to be mere progression of colours, acquires an imagist significance and takes upon itself the task of expressing emotional shades.

Then the colour scale, whose laws of development permeate the objective appearance of coloured phenomena, will be an exact replica—in its own sphere—of the musical score emotionally colouring the events.

Then the gleam of a conflagration takes on a sinister character and the colour of red becomes thematic red.

Then cold blue checks the riot of orange patches echoing the freezing of the action at the beginning.

Then the yellow associated with sunlight and skilfully set out by blue sings the song of life and joy, coming after black streaked with red.

Then, finally, the theme expressed in colour *leit-motifs* can, through its colour score and with its own means, unfold an inner drama, weaving its own pattern in the contrapuntal whole, crossing and recrossing the course of action, which formerly music alone could do with full completeness by supplementing what could not be expressed by acting or gesture; it was music alone that could sublimate the inner melody of a scene into thrilling audio-visual atmosphere of a finished audio-visual episode.

I think that from the point of view of method the best thing would be to show such a principle in action on a concrete example.

So I shall give a short description of how the colour sequence was constructed in *Ivan the Terrible.**

1948

* The MS breaks off here.—*Ed.*

Shooting his Mexican film

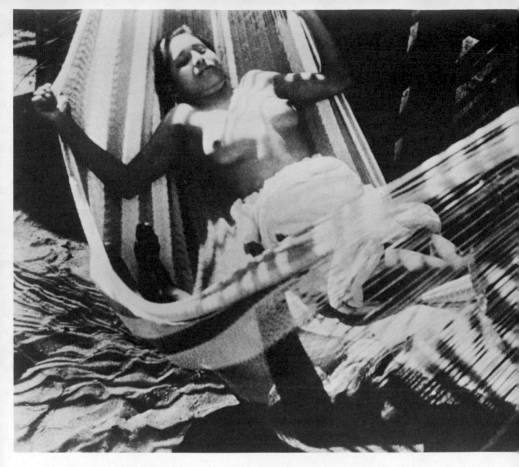

Shot from the hammock sequence in *¡Que Viva Mexico!*
(courtesy The Museum of Modern Art/Film Stills Archive)

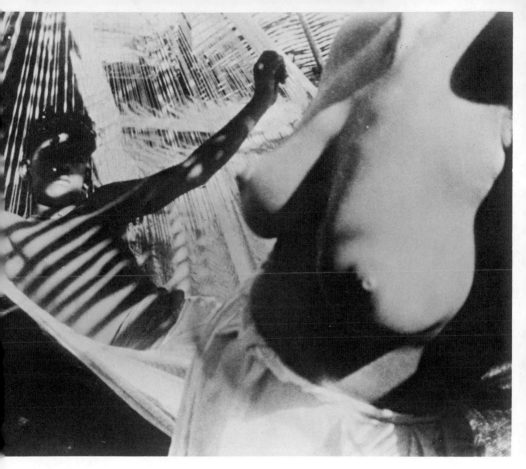

Shot from the hammock sequence in *¡Que Viva Mexico!*
(courtesy The Museum of Modern Art/Film Stills Archive)

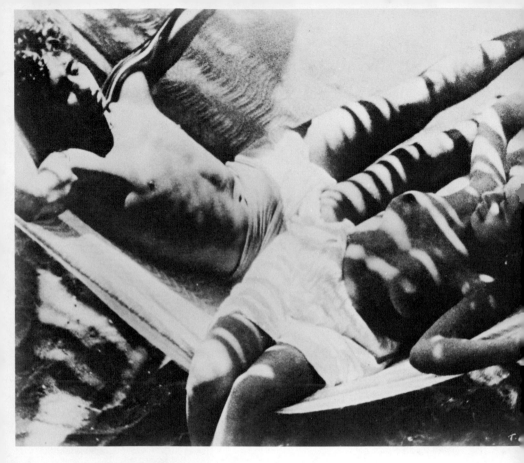

Shot from the hammock sequence in *¡Que Viva Mexico!*
(courtesy The Museum of Modern Art/Film Stills Archive)

Shot from *¡Que Viva Mexico!:* punishment of the revolu-
tionaries (courtesy The Museum of Modern Art/Film Stills
Archive)

Eisenstein setting up one of the final scenes from *¡Que Viva Mexico!* (courtesy The Museum of Modern Art/Film Stills Archive)

STEREOSCOPIC FILMS

Today you meet many people who ask, "Do you believe in stereoscopic films?"

Asking this question, I think, is as senseless as asking me if I believe that two comes after one, or that snow melts in spring, or that trees are green in summer and apples ripen in autumn.

It is as naïve to doubt that the stereoscopic film is the tomorrow of the cinema as it is to doubt that tomorrow will come.

Why are we so sure about it? All we have seen so far on the screen is merely lone Robinsonades.

Is it not symbolic that the best among these is precisely the screen version of the story of Robinson Crusoe?*

And yet what we see here is nothing more than Robinson's raft shown in the picture as it tries to slip past the tangled lianas (one of the best stereoscopic shots in Andrievsky's film), which symbolized, as it were, the hosts of difficulties we had yet to overcome in stereoscopic films.

But the day is near when instead of rafts, we shall see galleys, frigates, cruisers, battleships and dreadnoughts arriving in stereoscopic film ports.

Why are we so confident?

Because I think that only those forms of art are viable whose very essence provides an outlet to the cherished aspirations inherent in human nature itself. The important thing is not only the subject of a work of art but also by what means of its particular forms it is expressed.

It is quite possible that the survival of certain forms of art is governed by the same law of natural selection as that prevailing in other spheres of life.

The art "species" that survive are those whose structure accords with the innermost organic tendencies and requirements of both the creator and the spectator.

The deeper the requirements and the more fully they are satisfied,

---

* *Robinson Crusoe*, produced by A. N. Andrievsky, was one of the first Soviet stereoscopic films.—*Ed.*

the more reason there is that a given form of art will exist, the more ground that it will develop.

Are we not witnessing the inevitable and inexorable decay of the so-called "pure," abstract art because it does not satisfy the inner urge for knowledge inherent in every progressive-minded person?

This art appeared and could exist for a short period as a reflection of the decadence of the doomed social class that engendered it.

It could not become an independent "species" or form of art, capable of developing, changing in form and growing, and did not prove worthy of taking its place beside other art forms.

And yet there is a no less "abstract" form of art that has existed almost unchanged for centuries—the circus.

That is because, without attempting to trespass on the sphere of knowledge with which other arts are coping more successfully, the feats of dexterity, strength, self-possession, volitional purposefulness and daring one sees at the circus, will always be in keeping with men's inborn striving for the fullest possible development of these qualities, a striving rooted deep in human nature.

The same reason determines the popularity of sports, both with the athletes and the fans, for it provides us with the broadest scope and most perfect forms of exercising and developing our natural faculties, not only as spectators but as active participants.

Can it be said that the three-dimensional principle in the stereoscopic film fully and consecutively answers some inner urge, that it satisfies some inborn requirement of human nature?

Can it be said further that, in striving to realize this urge, humanity for centuries has been heading for the stereoscopic film as a complete and direct expression of this striving, a striving which, at different stages of social development and evolution of artistic means of expression, invariably and persistently tended to realize some inner urge though in different ways and incompletely?

I think it can.

I should like to try to explain the nature of this urge by examining the various methods with which the arts of former times realized this urge before it could be done most graphically and fully with the aid of the technical miracle of the stereoscopic film.

Let us try to establish what inner urge of the spectator can be expressed by the technical phenomenon of the stereoscopic film. We know that by its very nature the motion picture possesses its own independent attraction in that it is endowed with the main characteristic of life on earth, of humanity and progress—movement!

In the first place we must characterize the nature of the phenomenon under discussion.

A few words about the thing that strikes one most on seeing a stereoscopic film for the first time.

Stereoscopic films produce an illusion that their representations are three-dimensional.

The illusion is complete and arouses no more doubt in the spectator than does the fact that representations on the screen actually move in the ordinary films. The illusion of volume in the former instance and of movement in the latter is equally indisputable for those who are perfectly aware that in one case we have a moving sequence of separate motionless phases taken from an unbroken process of movement and in the other, a skilful superimposition of two ordinary, flat photographic representations of one object, synchronically photographed from two slightly different angles.

In both cases the results are as spatially and dynamically convincing and undeniably perfect as the characters of the film are seemingly real and living, although we know very well that they are no more than pale shadows impressed by photo-chemical means on miles of gelatin strip which, in the shape of reels, is conveyed in cans from one end of the globe to another, everywhere amazing the spectators with the illusion of real life.

There are three kinds of stereoscopic effect. The representation stays within the boundaries of the conventional cinema; it looks like a flat high relief suspended on the surface of the screen.

Or the representation recedes deep into the screen, drawing the spectator into unknown depths.

Or the representation (and in this instance the effect is overwhelming) perceived in its three dimensions "falls" out of the screen into the auditorium.

A cobweb with an enormous spider seems to be suspended between the screen and the spectator.

Birds fly from the auditorium *into* the screen or settle quietly over the heads of the audience on wires tangibly stretching from what used to be the surface of the screen to the projector.

Branches of trees hang over the audience.

Panthers and pumas leap out of the screen frame at the audience, and so on.

The representation obtained may expand and recede deep into the screen producing the effect of space, or seem material, three-dimensional, tangible and moving on the audience—the effect of dimension. All that depends on the difference in calculating the angle when photographing.

What we have become accustomed to see represented on the flat surface of the screen suddenly "swallows us up" and draws us into the inside-the-screen space we never saw before, or "pierces" us with unprecedented force.

Like colour, that new phase of colour expressiveness, compared with the white, grey and black palette of the old films, stereoscopy is a new and more perfect phase in the development of the tendencies which manifested themselves in the cinema in its "two-dimensional" period.

This tendency was particularly manifest in one of my favourite methods of composing shots, first of all, those representing nature.

This method consisted (and consists) in bringing the close-up of the foreground as sharply forward as possible and maintaining simultaneously the background in focus, softened only to the extent required by the aerial perspective to create the greatest possible contrast between the "depth" and the foreground.

Maximum illusion of space was achieved through the sensation of the vast difference in the size of the foreground and the "depth."

This was facilitated by the distorting property of Lens 28 which emphasized the "vanishing" perspective; it is the only lens capable of simultaneously presenting in focus very large details of the foreground and the depth of the background.

Such composition is highly effective both in cases where the two planes are thematically opposed and where they are unified.

In the first instance, this composition allows the greatest conflict of volume and space obtainable within a single shot.

In the second, it expresses with utmost plastic clarity the sense of unity between the general and the particular.

The greatest dramatic effect this composition produces, however, is in cases when it unifies the two possibilities, when, say, the thematic unity of the two planes is solved and their plastic. (scale, colour) incommensurability is emphasized simultaneously.

It was in this way that the final shots of *Ivan the Terrible*, Part I, were solved. Indeed, the most impressive shot in that sequence was that of the boundless expanse of snow with a religious procession moving in the background, and the close-up of the Tsar's profile in the foreground.

The shot, thematically unifying the people who implore the tsar to come back and Ivan who gives his consent, is plastically solved by means of the greatest possible plastic (scale and colour) contrast of the two "objects."

...It is noteworthy that the composition of the above-mentioned examples from non-stereoscopic films has so far proved more effective than the purely technical achievements of the stereoscopic cinema.

That is because the technical possibilities of the latter are fettered by the necessity of our using Lens 50 and this lens is one of the least expressive.

At the same time we foresee that stereoscopy's potentialities will with time give us new, unheard-of qualities in the sphere of expressiveness.

Be as it may, the stereoscopic film has given us two spatial possibilities which, though not yet fully expressive, are perceived as physically real. These are the ability to "draw" the audience with unprecedented force into what used to be a flat surface and the ability to "bring down" on the audience that which formerly spread over the surface of the screen.

"Well," one may ask, "what of it? Why should these two 'wonderful possibilities' of the stereoscopic screen prove specially attractive to the spectator?"

...And of course no other art has ever furnished an example of so dynamic and perfect transition of volume into space, space into volume, of their splicing and coexisting, and all that in the process of real motion.

In this respect the stereoscopic film is superior even to architecture where the majestic symphony of interplaying massifs and spatial outlines, whose dynamics and succession depend on the tempo and order of the spectator's progress through the architectural whole, can lend dynamics to it only through his own motion.

... Since the stereoscopic cinema is an entertainment art, it must be recognized not only as a direct outcome of the inventions of Edison and Lumière but also as an off-shoot of the theatre, of which it constitutes, in its present form, the newest and latest evolutionary phase.

The secret of the effectiveness of the stereoscopic film principle (if it does possess it) must be sought for in one of the main trends present in almost all the periods of the history of the theatre.

... But of all the various problems of the theatre the one I am most interested in is that of relations between and interdependence of the spectacle and the spectator.

... And the curious thing is that almost immediately after the splitting into the spectator and the performer there appeared an urge to reunite these two divorced halves.

This urge has appeared not only in the works of conscious authors who prosper in the epoch when individualism has reached its apogee, not only in numberless practical experiments characteristic of our days—that is, in the attempts to realize this tendency towards the re-establishment of the original "common nature" of performances, but throughout the history of the theatre whose countless examples of past stage techniques, for centuries, everywhere, reveal the invariable striving for the realization of this one and the same sharp tendency towards the bridging of the "chasm" separating the actor from the spectator.

These attempts range from the "coarse and material" external methods of planning the place of action and the place allotted to the spectators, and the stage behaviour of the actors, to the most refined "symbolic" realization of this dream of the union of the spectator and the actor.

The tendency to go over to the spectator and the tendency to draw the spectator onto the stage have invariably existed side by side,

134

either competing or developing parallel to each other, as if foreshadowing the two specific possibilities lying in the technical nature of what we have designated as the chief plastic characteristic (the main optical phenomenon) of the stereoscopic film.

...The bourgeois West treats the problem of stereoscopy in the cinema either with indifference or with scorn, but the researchers and inventors in the Land of Soviets, its government and its leading filmdom officials pay a great deal of attention to it.

Isn't the stagnant conservatism, with which the news of the work on stereoscopic films is received in the West, absurd and even insulting to the tendency towards perpetual development inherent in all true art?

Didn't the following words of Louis Chavance sound sacrilegious and smacking of obscurantism in July 1946?

Here they are: "What does dramatism of situations gain from this new technical discovery?

"Does a three-dimensional comedian find any additional means of expression in this third dimension?

"Such as physical roundness?

"Will this be the triumph of the fat man?

"What do wrath, jealousy, hate stand to gain from being unfolded in three dimensions?

"What about laughter?... I don't think anything can provoke more laughter than the custard-pies thrown into the faces of Mack Sennett's 'flat' characters. What about the plot? And comedy?

"Need it be further proved that the stereoscopic film is a useless tool, a sterile instrument?

"Of course other hypotheses could be advanced. I could speak of its purely spectacular aspect. But we must not make an analogy with the plastic arts and quote sculptors after discussing painters. Of course, the life of Michelangelo could be filmed in relief as well as the life of Titian in colour. With a very charming result! What a feast for the eye! The sculpture would appear tangible, but we still would not touch the screen."

Where is Chavance wrong? In that while posing as an enemy of analogies he is actually their slave; he is a slave of the ideas and notions of old arts, of the laws of the drama, of the actor's technique and of "sculpture appearing tangible."

But doesn't he think, as we do, that there will be an explosion, a complete revision of the cooperation of the traditional arts as a result of the conflict with the new ideologies of the new times, with the new potentialities of the new people, with the new methods these people possess of influencing nature?

Aren't the eyes capable of seeing in the dark with the aid of infra-red glasses; aren't the hands capable of guiding missiles and aircraft from a very great distance by means of radio; isn't the brain capable, with the help of electronic computers, of calculating within a few seconds something that used to require months of work on the part of a whole army of accountants; isn't the consciousness, waging an incessant struggle since the end of the war, shaping a concrete image of a truly democratic international ideal; doesn't all this demand absolutely new arts of unheard-of forms and dimensions, arts that should leave far behind all such palliatives as the traditional theatre, traditional sculpture and traditional ... cinema?

And won't the new, dynamic, stereoscopic sculpture overstep the dimensions and peculiarities of the old, static sculpture, whose standards Chavance tries to apply to it?

We should not be afraid of the coming era.

To say nothing of laughing in its face, as our forefathers were apt to do when they flung mud at the first umbrellas.

We should prepare our consciousness for the coming of new themes which, multiplied by the potentialities of new techniques, will demand a new aesthetics for skilfully realizing these new themes in the new, breath-taking works of the future.

To clear the way for them is a sacred duty which must be performed by all who call themselves artists.

The only ones who fail to believe in the victory of the new potentialities of the technique of tomorrow are those who do not believe in tomorrow, in the first place those who are deprived of a tomorrow by history, those who deny the fruitfulness of further social development of nations, those who are active stemming it, and those who in the face of the future that will inevitably destroy them are desperately clinging to all that is reactionary and conservative, seeing in it the only guarantee of preserving the bourgeois-capitalist system that is so dear to their hearts.

We are not like them, our country is different.

We are always striving for new and new achievements!

We are always mastering new techniques!

We are always perfecting the future techniques of expressing our ideas.

For the glorious, triumphant and brilliant tomorrow is ours!

It belongs to us and to those who have joined us in leading mankind towards a bright future!

1947-48

PORTRAITS
OF ARTISTS

THE GREATEST CREATIVE HONESTY

I met Gorky several times during the last years of his life. Those were exciting, never-to-be-forgotten meetings. I cherish their memory all the more now that they can never be repeated. What diverse interests Gorky had! How mildly ironic, and at times scathingly sarcastic he was when talking of an enemy or a renegade! How capably he could snatch from life the most typical and characteristic feature of a phenomenon! How full were his memories of personal contacts with men who for our generation are classics! What wonderful knowledge he had of folk-lore!

This greatest of proletarian writers said many things which I will never forget.

But here I would like to speak of the trait which has a special significance for our era of artistic unpretentiousness. This trait is the astonishing modesty of the departed giant of creative thought.

This modesty was no pose but an inborn quality, the extremely precious characteristic of Gorky the man, creator and artist. His modesty was an integral part of his creative honesty and sense of responsibility. This quality of Gorky's has remained in my memory as an immense "close-up," to use film terminology.

It happened early in the summer of 1934. Some of us intimate friends of Gorky had got together and he was telling us about his plans for a film scenario about children during the Civil War years and the period of the re-education of homeless children.* He strongly disapproved of the films that had been made, but instead of criticizing them, he wanted to make a different, a true work. It was then that I discovered in him a trait at once extremely touching and grand. We young men, ardent admirers of his talent, burnt with impatience and enthusiasm as we realized that the great master had chosen us to read his new work to. He was even more excited than we. He fingered the pages of the MS before he began reading in his muffled yet booming voice. The fingers of Gorky, a writer of world fame, the classic of today, his fingers *were trembling.* This excitement at the moment when he was parting with his brain-child, at the moment when it was passing from him to millions of listeners and readers (represented by us), this excitement was unforgettable evidence of the profound responsibility this truly great artist felt for each of his creative efforts.

I do not wish to emphasize this characteristic by any contrasts. There are too many of them around us and in our very midst. And in too many instances the respect for our Russian people, to which we have dedicated our efforts and together with which we are marching towards historic victories, is not sufficiently strong and genuine. May Gorky's trembling fingers holding the leaves of the MS remind us that honesty and modesty are inseparable in an artist.

Much more could be added. But I prefer to cut my story short, just as Gorky cut short his address to the meeting at the Byelo-

* Eisenstein means the script of *Delinquents* on which Gorky worked in 1932.—*Ed.*

russian Station where many thousands came to welcome him home from abroad. "I cannot speak," he said with tears in his eyes, "I'll write. . . ."

We have no choice but to write, as we realize with bitterness that we shall never be able to speak to him again. But his voice will resound throughout centuries in his works.

1936

THE BIRTH OF AN ARTIST

That is a wonderful moment in the life of every artist, the moment when you realize that you have become an artist, that you have been recognized as an artist.

I have but a vague recollection of how this happened to me.

Although I have experienced this on three occasions.

I believe the most forceful of the experiences was the one I lived through in 1923 when, at a Bolshoi Theatre jubilee performance, I staged a fragment of my first production. (It was Ostrovsky's *Enough Simplicity in Every Wise Man* and I appeared on the bill for the first time as a director.) At the preview on the eve of the performance the fragment seemed a complete failure. But there could be no question of taking it off the programme. And among the audience there would be some of the biggest names in the theatre! A horrible night. Maddening anxiety during the day. Terrible panic in the evening. And all of a sudden in the middle of the performance, applause shook the auditorium. Yes, the house was shaken. I can find no better word to describe the sudden outburst that reverberated throughout the hall. It was shaken once. Then again. And then the thunder rolled until the curtain was rung down. No, I was so astounded by this unexpected success that I forgot to ring the curtain down. I remembered it several minutes later.

For many years I kept the suit with a yawning hole near one of the coat pockets. The suit was new, too. I wore it for the first time that evening. I don't remember where I ripped my coat as I staggered to a seat after the curtain had come down. I preserved the coat as a relic. It was to remind me of the night when my audience proclaimed me a director.

I lived through a still more significant event—the *première* of *Potemkin,* held at the Bolshoi Theatre two years later to commemorate the twentieth anniversary of the 1905 Revolution.

But you experience even greater exaltation at the birth of a new artist whose first steps coincide with his coming into the world as a creative personality.

"Do come and see the new film they have sent us," a representative of the Ukrainian Film Studios pleaded over the telephone. "We can't make head or tail of it; it's called *Zvenigora.*"

The auditorium of the Hermitage Theatre in Karetny Ryad was an oblong box with mirrored walls. In addition to the real screen you see two more reflected in the mirrors. It would be hard indeed to find anything worse for a cinema auditorium.

Near the entrance, at a small table, sat Zuyev-Insarov. For a ruble he analyzed your handwriting. For three rubles he sent his findings in a sealed envelope to your home. A little way off, in the centre of a flower-bed, was a cast-iron bust of Pushkin. Every summer it was painted differently. One year it gleamed like a black lacquered car, and the next it was a dull whitish grey in keeping with the garden benches.

We proceeded to the Mirror Auditorium where the strange film was to be shown. The man from the Ukrainian Film Studios who had telephoned me got at me again.

"Help us, please. Tell us frankly what you think of it!"

The young Ukrainian director's baptism was taking place under a good roof.

Under an historic roof: it was here, too, that the Art Theatre staged its first performance—Chekhov's *Seagull.*

And here also many masters of the conventional theatre started their careers.

I was very proud of having begun my theatrical biography in 1920 here: I staged my first work, *The Mexican,* at this theatre.

Pudovkin and I took our seats. We were then just making a name for ourselves. *Potemkin* and *Mother* had been released less than a year before that and had just had their run of the globe.

A hasty introduction to the director of *Zvenigora*, Alexander Dovzhenko.

Zvenigora was shown on three screens at once—one real and two mirrors.

Goodness gracious, what a sight!

We saw sharp-keeled boats sailing out of double exposures.

The rump of a black stallion being painted white.

A horrible monk with a lantern being either disinterred or buried—I am not sure which.

The audience were whispering, their curiosity stung.

And the thought uppermost in my mind was that after the show I'd have to describe my impressions; I'd have to say something clever....

For an "expert" this is a sort of test. And meanwhile the film galloped on the three screens and they made it look still more fantastic.

We saw "grandpa"—symbolizing the old—instigated by his villainous son, putting dynamite on the rails over which a train—the symbol of progress—was to pass.

Travelling in the train was "grandpa's" other son, one of us, a good Soviet citizen. He sat drinking tea. But no catastrophe occurred.

And all of a sudden "grandpa"—the symbol of the old—was shown in a third-class compartment, just an ordinary old man, drinking tea with his son from an ordinary teapot.

Perhaps I've made a mess of the plot—I am almost sure I have and hope Alexander will forgive me for it—but I remember very well the impression all this made on me, and here I am quite positive.

We felt we were succumbing to the irresistible charm of the picture. To the charm that lay in its original ideas, in the wonderful picture of what was real and what was a profoundly national poetic invention, of contemporaneity and legend, of the humorous and pathetic. In some way reminiscent of Gogol.

The next morning, still under the influence of the film, I began an article which I called *Red Hoffmann*, owing to this mixture of the real and fantastic. But I did not finish it. All that was left of the article were three narrow strips of paper covered with writing in red ink (at that time I wrote in red ink out of principle), full of enthusiasm for the daring combination of reality and imagist poetry in which lay the charm of the young artist's first work.

But that was to be on the following morning. Now, the three screens reflected three black rectangles with the words *The End.* Reddish electric bulbs returned reluctantly to life. And I saw a sea of eyes around me.

The show was over. The audience rose silently. But the atmosphere was tense with a feeling that a new talent had appeared in film art.

A talent with an original personality. A talent in his own *genre.* A talent with his own ego.

And at the same time our own. One of us. Our friend. A direct heir to the best traditions of Soviet cinema. A talent who did not beg for alms from West-minded film-makers.

As the lights went on, we all felt that we had just witnessed a memorable event in the development of the cinema. The man before us had created something new.

I was standing beside Pudovkin. We were faced with an unusual task: in answer to the expectant glances of the audience we had to give utterance to the feelings which gripped all but which—because of the strangeness of the event—it was very difficult to express. We had to say that we had just seen a remarkable film and met an even more remarkable man; and be the first to congratulate him.

And when Dovzhenko, an astonishingly slender man, indeed, slim as a reed and holding himself unusually upright, although not very young in years, when that man approached us with a self-conscious smile, Pudovkin and I warmly clasped his hand, rejoicing as much as we did thirteen years later when we congratulated him for his wonderful *Shchors.*

That is how Dovzhenko was "ordained" a director. On that day Diogenes's lantern could be extinguished: we had found a real man. A real, new and mature film producer. A real original trend within Soviet cinematography.

*   *   *

We celebrated the *première* of *Zvenigora* somewhat later—the day *Arsenal* was released. The three of us met on the topmost floor (recently added to the former Lianozov house) of the Committee of Cinematography, at 7, Maly Gnezdnikovsky Lane. That was at the time I was editing *Old and New*. Yet I set apart one evening in order to meet Dovzhenko informally for the first time. The two Moscow directors—Pudovkin and I—were keenly interested in the ideas and character of their new friend from Kiev. He, too, seemed to be on his guard. But very soon all restraint and conversation on "lofty subjects" were sent to the devil—we were still young enough, and at that age people use words only to give vent to the feelings crowding in their breasts.

The atmosphere of this "picnic" under the Sovkino roof had too much of the "student element" in it to encourage formality.

An improvised table was set up between the cutting-room and the projection-room. On the table we had bottles of mineral water and some sandwiches. We engaged in a heated exchange of opinions on the burning cinema problems in hurried staccato sentences. We felt young and surging with the creative energy of a new Renaissance. And we saw a perspective of boundless creative possibilities in the future.

We were in a big official building.... Our predecessors were great masters of culture.... And just as people don masks at carnivals, so did we, the three young directors intoxicated with the wonders of their art, draw lots for the characters of three giants of the past. I was to impersonate Leonardo da Vinci, Dovzhenko—Michelangelo, and Pudovkin, gesticulating excitedly, proclaimed he wanted to be Raphael. Yes, Raphael, who "by the beauty and refinement of his manner captivated all he met." Jumping off his chair, Pudovkin energetically impersonated the irresistible native of Urbino. But he was more like Flaubert when the latter, using a table-cloth as a train, tried to show to Emile Zola how the Empress Eugénie walked at the balls given by Napoleon III.

The make-shift table, chairs and stools were overturned and Leonardo da Vinci, Michelangelo and Raphael tried to outdo each other in what was left of their skill in gymnastics. Pudovkin showed how he could jump over chairs.

And the party ended very much like one of Chekhov's stories with the office-cleaner, pail and mop in hand, entering the room and stopping short as if rooted to the floor in his astonishment.

That is how we celebrated the appearance of *Zvenigora* and *Arsenal*.

1940

TWENTY-FIVE AND FIFTEEN

He is a year older than I am. But he has been in the films ten years longer. He was grinding the camera at a time when I did not even suspect I would be a film worker. He was already shooting pictures when I first felt the attraction of this form of entertainment and was infatuated with *Cabiria*, Max Linder, Pockson* and Prince, never thinking that this infatuation would go beyond platonic love.

First the war and then the Revolution determined his career: he was acknowledged the best of Soviet cameramen. These events sealed his fate. My life was reshaped by the Revolution and the Civil War: the career of a civil engineer took a sharp turn and became the career of a designer at front-line theatres and a director of the first workers' theatre in Moscow.

The logical development of my activities brought me to the cinema in 1924. The seething lava of searchings in the theatre, the ardent quest for the most effective means of emotionally impressing the audience, the unbridled ardour in the fight against established creative traditions—all that had attracted me to the theatre overstepped its boundaries and brought me to the cinema. Or rather flung me violently into the arms of one who had a fiery temperament, who had swept with his camera over all the fronts of the Civil War, over the spots where industry, at last the property of the people, was being rehabilitated.

The possessor of this temperament was a remarkably quiet and shy young man, hatless and in a white linen coat.

* "Pockson" was simply the name used by the Russian distributor for John Bunny. —*Ed.*

That is how Eduard Tisse looked when I first met him in the sun-dappled little garden of the house in Vozdvizhenka which once belonged to Morozov and which now housed our theatre.

Boris Mikhin, the manager of the film studio, had selected Tisse as the best partner for me.

"Your theatre goes in for acrobatics. I think you'll indulge in tricks in the cinema as well. Eduard has a brilliant record in newsreel work and he is a very good ... sportsman. I'm sure you two will get along fine," he said.

And we did. It is fifteen years now that we have been working together.

Thanks to Mikhin's intuition and foresight: he could not have chosen a better pair.

Our first talk was very brief. Tisse looked through the first script of *Strike* which I intended shooting. Then he explained that what I called "fade-in over fade-in" was known technically as "double exposure."

And in the evening he came to the theatre in order to see what kind of a director he would have to deal with. This visit nearly cost him his life.

Our version of Ostrovsky's *Wise Man* had a tightrope number performed by Grigory Alexandrov who was then known under the professional name of Mormonenko, a name to which he was partly entitled by right of descent. That evening the wire broke and one of the heavy metal platforms it was attached to fell with a clang, narrowly missing our chief cameraman to be. A chair beside him was smashed to pieces. Here for the first time we had occasion to admire Eduard's imperturbability: he did not even start. In these past fifteen years I have had many an occasion to see how cool and collected he is under the most trying circumstances.

He is invariably self-possessed and quick as the devil himself. Unquenchably temperamental and painstakingly pedantic, he is quick to grasp the facts but can be patient and persevering in his quest for the needed effect. He is phenomenally hardy—among icebergs and in the sands, in the murky mists of the North and in the tropics, in Mexico, in the bull-fight arena, on stormy seas, in pits, under passing tanks—everywhere he has proved himself to be in no way inferior to stevedores, ploughmen, miners, underground builders. That man combines a feature he has in common with the finest masters of the plastic art, the sense of even imperceptible nuances, of the infinitesimal shade in his material, which, it is claimed, engenders true art, with huge, bony hands and sharp blue eyes. This is symbolic of the combination of the finest and most precise mental equipment and the ability to bear any hardship in order to realize his ideas.

I don't think there is anyone with whom I have discussed the cinema less than with Eduard.

It has been a tradition with us since our first laconic talk.

Does a man discuss things with his eye? He just sees with it.

Does a man say to his heart, "You must beat rhythmically"? It just beats by itself.

Does a man discuss with his chest how it should heave when he is excited?

I don't think the world has known another instance of such unity of seeing, feeling and experiencing as existed between Tisse and myself.

In the fifteen years we have worked together we have not substituted the familiar "thou" for the formal "you." The intimate form, I think, would have proved a parody of the truly intimate relations we both are conscious of.

It is this inner intimacy which, after we have been running in opposite directions in search of a landscape, brings us to the one and only point from which we shoot it for the screen.

It is this inner intimacy which suggests to us a solution of a frame which in equal measure accords with the director's and the cameraman's conception.

It is this inner intimacy which maintains the line of unerring stylistic unity through the vicissitudes of the shooting and precludes the possibility of any potential montage shot-piece being a plastic "dissonance," whenever and wherever it may be shot.

And finally, this creative intimacy is responsible for what we value most in our method of shooting.

Whatever we may be shooting, be it pre-revolutionary factories, the Petersburg of Rastrelli, warships at sea, plough-lands and meadows, palms, cactuses, pyramids, helmets, breastplates, spears, or a thirteenth-century ice-covered lake, we always look for one and the same thing in our shots.

It is neither something unexpected nor decorative. Nor an unusual angle. It is the greatest possible expressiveness.

And everywhere beyond representations we look for a generalized image of the phenomenon we are shooting.

In order to achieve this generalized image we search for a suitable shot, a suitable camera angle, a suitable composition within the frame and in this search we constantly and persistently change the position of the camera, moving it, extending or contracting the beam, trying the shot with all the lenses and filters at our disposal.

The unity of the visible form of an object and of its imagist generalization, achieved by means of the composition of the shot, is to us the most important feature of a truly realistic treatment of the shot. We consider that this ensures the emotional impression which the sight of the purely plastic images on the screen can excite. This imagist treatment of representations is the most important task the cameraman has; in fulfilling it, he permeates all the minutest details of the plastic solution of the film with the theme and his attitude to the theme.

We have not made any statements on the essence of our method. We did not spend nights smoking countless cigarettes as we worked it out.

But in the fifteen years that we have been working hand in hand we have striven for it, looking for it in the environments, and trying enthusiastically to grasp events in all their variety. Those parts and plastic elements of our films where our quest has been fruitful are marked by success.

This, finally, enabled us for the first time to achieve complete harmony between representation and music—as may be seen in *Alexander Nevsky*. Here the emotional "music of representation" and of landscape, the "not indifferent nature" we have been striving for all through the years of our work, effortlessly harmonize with the highly plastic elements which abound in Prokofiev's highly emotional music. The meeting with Prokofiev brought Eduard and me as much creative joy as did our own meeting fifteen years ago. In Prokofiev we found the ally we had sought for our campaign of conquest of the sound film.

Eisenstein and Eduard Tisse (1925)

Sergei Eisenstein listens as Sergei Prokofiev plays the
music for *Ivan the Terrible*

Rereading the foregoing paragraphs I see that I have written as much about myself as about Tisse. But this does not frighten me: when Tisse writes about me on the occasion of my silver jubilee in the cinema, which will also be the twenty-fifth anniversary of our work together and the thirty-fifth anniversary of his work, he will have to say as much about himself as about me.

And that will make me very happy, for it will prove that we have worked together through another decade of as close a creative friendship as that of the fifteen years in the past.

1939

P—R—K—F—V

"You'll have the music by twelve noon."

We leave the small projection-room. Although it is now midnight. I feel quite calm. I know that at exactly 11.55 a. m. a small, dark blue car will bring Sergei Prokofiev to the studio and that in his hands there will be the necessary piece of music for *Alexander Nevsky*.

At night we look through a new sequence of the film.

By morning a new sequence of music will be ready for it.

*　　*　　*

Prokofiev works like a clock.

This clock neither gains nor loses time.

Like a sniper it hits the very heart of punctuality. Prokofiev's punctuality is not a matter of business pedantry.

His punctuality is a by-product of creative exactitude.

Of absolute exactitude in transposing musical imagery into a mathematically exact means of expression, which Prokofiev has harnessed with a bridle of steel.

This is the exactitude of Stendhal's laconic style translated into music.

In crystal purity of expressive language Prokofiev is equalled only by Stendhal.

A century ago Stendhal said: *"Je mets un billet dans une loterie dont le gros lot se réduit à ceci: être lu en 1935"*;* although it is hard for us now to believe that there was a generation that did not see the lucidity of Stendhal's style.

Prokofiev is luckier.

His works will not have to wait a hundred years to be recognized. Prokofiev is widely recognized, both at home and abroad.

This process has been speeded up by his association with the cinema. Not merely because this association has popularized his work through the plots of the films, the large number of copies of each film, or the wide popularity of the cinema.

But because Prokofiev's art is something behind the surface appearance of an event—something similar to what an event must pass through in the film process.

It must first pass through the lens, in order to become a film representation which, pierced by the blinding ray of the projector, will live a new and magic life of its own on the white surface of the screen.

*   *   *

I have always been intrigued by the "mystery" of the birth of a musical image, the emergence of melodies** and appearance of that captivating harmony and unity which arise from the chaos of the temporary correlations and disconnected sounds that fill the world around the composer.

On this score I share the curiosity of my praiseworthy driver Grigory Zhurkin.

As my chauffeur he has seen pictures filmed, cut, projected and rehearsed.

"I know all about film production," he says. "I have seen all and

---

* "I have drawn a lottery ticket and the prize is this: to be read in 1935."—*Tr.*
** The fact that a melody often is not "invented" but borrowed from external, say, folk-lore sources, does not change the matter. Because the composer chooses from among the wealth of melodies and themes only such as appeal to him, such as can set his imagination on fire, that is, those that satisfy his inner craving for expression. Consequently, the "choice" of a melody in this sense in no way differs from the "creation" of one.—*Author's Note.*

I know all. The only thing I can't understand is how Sergei Sergeye-vich* writes music!"

This problem had long given me no rest, too, until one day I got a good peep into his creative process.

Leaving aside for the time being the broader problems of this process, let us see how Prokofiev's mind shapes the seemingly non-related material presented to him into a distinct and logical composition.

The curious thing about this is that I succeeded in catching a glimpse of this process as I watched him... memorize telephone numbers, not write music.

This observation struck me so forcibly that I penned it under a typically detective headline: "The Telephone Betrays."

The notes in question were written down on the night of December 31, 1944, between 10 and 11 p.m., before I left for the Film Workers' Club. Here they are.

THE TELEPHONE BETRAYS

New Year 1945 is only a few hours away.

I phone Prokofiev to wish him a Happy New Year.

I dial K 5-10-20, extension 35, without consulting my telephone book.

I have a pretty good memory.

Perhaps because I do my best not to clutter it with such trifles as telephone numbers.

These I cross out from my memory and jot down in a miniature grey notebook.

How was it, then, that I remembered so easily the phone of Prokofiev's new apartment where he had moved so recently?

K 5-10-20, extension 35.

Why did the number engrave itself so firmly in my memory?

...Prokofiev was sitting next to me in a sound booth. He had just told me he had at last moved from a hotel to a new apartment.

* Prokofiev.—*Tr.*

On Mozhaisk Highway.

An apartment with gas.

And a telephone.

The orchestra were blasting away the clear-cut sequences of what was known as "Ivan Imploring the Boyars."

On the screen Nikolai Cherkasov (as Ivan the Terrible) goes down on his knees, imploring the boyars to swear allegiance to the lawful heir—Dimitry—so as not to expose Russia to the danger of new invasions and prevent her from breaking up into rivalling feudal principalities.

If you have seen the film you probably remember the episode for the unique harmony between movement and music with the double-basses predominating.

Of the canons ensuring this harmony between music and representation I have had occasion to write much and in detail.

The solution of the riddle was supplied by my work with Prokofiev on *Alexander Nevsky*.

But while working on *Ivan the Terrible* I was interested not in the *result* but in the *process* through which harmony is achieved.

I persistently sought to puzzle out how Prokofiev could manage, after seeing the rushes two or three times, to grasp the emotional mood, rhythm and structure of a scene and hand me *the musical equivalent* of the image, that is, the score, *on the next day*.

In the scene run for the tenth time for the rehearsing orchestra the effect was particularly striking. The music appeared to have been written for a finally edited sequence. And yet the composer had been given only the approximate length of the entire sequence.

Nevertheless, in the 60 metres of film we did not have to add or cut out a single shot, because all the necessary accents in music and action were wonderfully distributed.

More, they were not crudely synchronized but were intertwined in the complex texture of music and action in a much subtler way where synchronization was a rare and exceptional case necessitated by montage and the logic of action.

I pondered long and earnestly on that wonderful ability of Prokofiev's.

The orchestra had at last mastered the score. Conductor Stasevich was ready for the recording.

Sound engineer Volsky put on his ear-phones.

The sound apparatus was set in motion.

We sat staring at the screen, watching the birth of the audio-visual whole made up of the representation and the orchestra whose predecessor, the piano, used to blend the two so convincingly.

The music was recorded once.

Twice.

Thrice.

Four times.

The fifth recording was faultless.

The impetuous composer already had his checkered muffler around his neck.

There he was with his coat and hat on.

Hurriedly shaking my hand.

And, making for the door, giving me a phone number.

The number of his new flat:

"K 5-10-20, extension 35!"

And this betrayed his whole method.

That unravelled the mystery I was after.

Because this is how he pronounced the number:

"K. 5! 10!! 20!!! extension 30!!!! 5."

I have made use of a way of writing in the manner of early Khlebnikov in order to reproduce more exactly the *intonational crescendo* with which Prokofiev shouted the phone number to me.

"But," you may ask, "where is the key to the mystery of Prokofiev's creative process?"

I will make myself clear.

I am now dealing *not* with the creation of music and the wealth of images and sounds teeming in Prokofiev's head and heart (yes, this wisest of modern composers has a very warm heart). I am seeking a key only to the astonishing phenomenon of his being able to create a musical equivalent to any piece of visual incident projected on the screen.

There are diverse ways of memorizing things.

Association is very often one of them.

Sometimes the method is compositional (words one must remember become interlinked and produce a concrete picture in one's memory).

One's mnemonic methods often furnish the key to the nature of his mental processes.

Prokofiev's mnemonic method is astonishingly like, as one vaguely guesses, his method of perceiving the representation which he so unerringly translates into sounds.

Indeed, what does Prokofiev do?

A casual series of numbers—5, 10, 20, 30 he momentarily perceives as an *orderly* series.

This series of numbers is actually the sequence we all use in the familiar *conventional formula* representing an *increasing quantity* generally.

"Five-ten-twenty-thirty" is just like "one hundred, two hundred, three hundred."

But this orderly series is fixed in Prokofiev's mind not as a *speculation* but with an *emotion* which is blended with this formula.

His intonation does not mean merely growing *loudness* corresponding to the increasing quantity, nor is it an automatically memorized rhythm of the words expressing the phone number. Incidentally, this is exactly how most musicians memorize telephone numbers.*

The composer differed from the musicians in that he pronounced the numbers with an intonation of *growing delight*: five! ten!! twenty!!! thirty!!!! as if this meant that he had won thousands of rubles or shot as many snipe.

But of course there need not be an intonation of delight.

The intonation might be one of *fright*.

The motive for the emotional interpretation of the *order* espied in a series depends on the author and, in a case allowing different interpretations, may depend on any passing impression.

The intonation of delight with which Prokofiev pronounced his phone number might have been the result of his joy at finally settling down in a flat of his own on Mozhaisk Highway after years of living in hotels.

Let us for a moment forget Mozhaisk Highway and the telephone number.

And remember the crux of Prokofiev's creative mnemonics.

In the chaos of haphazard phenomena he can perceive order.

---

* Although I used to know one who memorized melodies by tying knots!— *Author's Note.*

Sergei Eisenstein and Vsevolod Pudovkin on the set of *Ivan the Terrible*

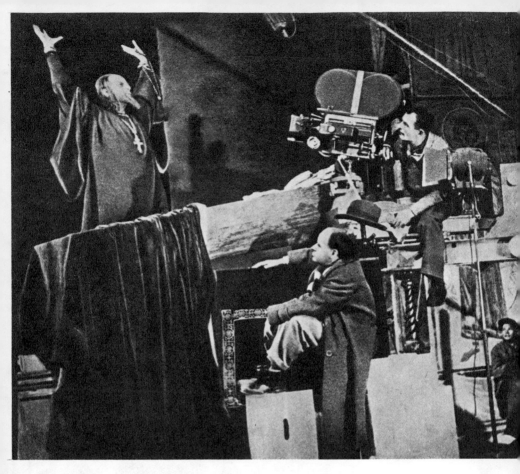

Filming *Ivan the Terrible*

The order discovered is emotionally interpreted.

And this emotional approach to a formula is unforgettable.

You just cannot forget it.

Telephone numbers are memorized through intonation.

And intonation is the basis of melody.

Prokofiev uses this method to derive intonations from the montage sequences following one another on the screen before him.

And intonation—the melody of speech "tune"—forms the basis of music!!

The story may be considered ended. We might add only that in the case of this method, both music and "visual" music, that is, the representation, must be composed on the same principle.

Here the experience of montage construction in the silent film comes in handy. The silent film demanded that music develop in the shot sequences along and in conformity with the narrative presentation of events.

And now, in the age of the sound film, we see that the montage of the silent era has made that method our second nature.

The repetition of an expressive combination of sounds, which is indispensable in music, is present in the rhythmical and montage groups of representations, too.

And we often see that a complete element of music, a "piece of phonogram" composed especially for a certain sequence of a scene, suits its other sequences to perfection.

The most remarkable thing about all this is that correspondence here generally does not affect major pieces alone or the general mood, but embraces the audio-visual "sprockets" in the pieces of representations and music, just as it does in the individual passage of the scene for which the music is originally composed.

I discussed this in regard to minor elements of articulation elsewhere, when I spoke about the Dawn Scene in *Alexander Nevsky*. I showed there in detail how *one and the same compositional scheme recurred in different spheres* of *plastic* possibilities.

An elaborate example of this can be seen in *Ivan the Terrible*, in the above-mentioned scene where Ivan implores the boyars to swear allegiance to Dimitry. In this instance the "phonogram" composed for *the first half* of the scene—before the entrance of Kurbsky—perfectly fits *the second half* of the episode.

And not only as regards duration: all synchronization and preconceived non-synchronization in the accents of action and music fit perfectly, too.

* * *

As a rule, Prokofiev and I bargain long and earnestly over "which is to be the first": whether he should write music for unedited pieces of representation which would then be edited accordingly, or I should complete the montage of a scene first and have music afterwards.

This is because the first has a more difficult task to solve: he must determine *the rhythmic course of the scene.*

The second has a "much easier" time.

He must erect an adequate "building" with the "building materials" of his own art.

The word "easier" must not be understood literally: it is "easier" only as compared with the first stage. I am pretty well familiar with the "inner mechanics" of the process.

It is a feverish kind of work but awfully thrilling.

To cope with it successfully, one must remember very distinctly all the plastic material to be dealt with.

Then one must have the recorded phonogram "run" an infinite number of times, patiently waiting for the moment when certain elements of one order suddenly start corresponding to certain elements of the other.

For instance, the texture of an object or a landscape and the timbre of a musical passage; the possibility of coordinating rhythmically a number of long shots with another musical passage; the rationally inexpressible "inner harmony" of a piece of music and a piece of representation, etc.

What makes all this difficult is the "chaotic state" of the pieces of representation. And, goaded by the inexorable laws of music, the "spirit of coordination" hovering over this primordial "chaos of representation" goes constantly from end to end, from piece to piece in order to determine how to juxtapose the pieces so that they harmonize with this or that passage of music.

One must bear in mind, too, that each piece of representation has its own canons which must never be lost sight of if the pieces are to be plastically *connected*!

Strictly speaking, this process does not differ in principle from what we do now in the era of audio-visual montage.

The only difference is that then we arranged the pieces of representation to correspond with the "score" we heard with our inner ear, and not with the incomparable music of Prokofiev.

For no montage can be accomplished if there is no inner "melody" to determine its construction!

This inner melody may resound so powerfully that sometimes it determines the rhythm of one's behaviour at the time one edits certain scenes.

For instance, I remember very well the "subdued" rhythm with which I did everything on the days I edited the "mists" and "mourning over Vakulinchuk" and the "sharp" rhythm on the days I edited the "Odessa steps" sequence. On this second occasion I walked in march tempo, treated my family harshly, spoke brusquely and *staccato*.

I cannot describe in detail this process in the composer's soul. And yet I have been able to catch a glimpse or two of how Prokofiev works.

* * *

I have always wondered how Prokofiev, knowing only the number of seconds allotted to him and having seen the edited material twice (or thrice, at the most), can have the music ready on the very next day, music which corresponds unerringly and precisely in all its *caesurae* and accents not only with the general rhythm of the entire episode, but with all the subtlest nuances of the montage development.

Correspondence here is not mechanical coincidence—that elementary instance of correspondence between pictures and music.

There is always the astonishing contrapuntal development of music which fuses with the representation.

I shall not expatiate here on the wonderful synaesthetic synchronization of the sounds with the image on the screen. That is an altogether independent subject dealing with another of Prokofiev's gifts—his ability to build up sound equivalents for the representations that come within his field of vision.

Any composer setting out to write music for the screen, as well as any director with an ambition to work in the sound film, to say nothing of the chromophone film (that is, a colour musical), must possess this ability, although not so highly developed as in the case of Prokofiev.

I shall confine myself at present to analyzing the methods by which Prokofiev finds structural and rhythmical equivalents for the edited pieces of film he works on.

The hall is plunged in darkness. But the darkness does not prevent me from seeing, in the patches of light coming from the screen, Prokofiev's hands on the elbow-rests of his chair, those enormous, strong hands with steel fingers which force the keyboard to groan when he attacks it with all the elemental impetuosity of his temperament.

Pictures flash on the screen. . . .

And the relentlessly precise, long fingers of Prokofiev are nervously drumming on the elbow-rests, as if receiving telegraph signals.

Is Prokofiev beating time?

No, he is "beating" something more complex.

His moving fingers grasp the structural canons governing the lengths of time and tempo in the edited pieces, harmonizing these with the actions and intonations of the characters.

I come to this conclusion on hearing him cry out, "Isn't that grand!" as he watches a piece with a cunning contrapuntal construction of three movements which do not coincide in rhythm, tempo and direction: protagonist, group background and poles flashing by in the foreground as the camera passes them.

Taking with him the structural canon of the scene in the rhythmical pattern his fingers have drummed out on the elbow-rests, on the following day he will send me the music which will permeate my montage structure with a similar sound counterpoint.

I seem to hear him muttering something or humming a tune.

God forbid you should address him at such a moment!

Instead of answering you he will either mutter incoherently (if your question has not penetrated his consciousness), or snap at you, or even curse you (if he has heard you).

What is it that Prokofiev listens to and hears within himself?

The answer in the present instance is more conjectural than in the former, and although graphic corroboration is harder to find here than there, I still think that the reply is a fairly convincing one.

I think that Prokofiev's muttering is the embryo of a melodic equivalent to the scene on the screen.

What are its component parts?

I think that, in addition to the drama itself and the situations which, being the decisive impressive factor, determine the most important aspect—the emotional-imagist nature and meaning of the episode, there are the intonational colouring of the actor's performance and the tonal (and in the colour film—tonal and colour) solution and progress of the scene.

It seems to me that it is precisely the tone and timbre of the representation that give birth to its melodic and orchestral equivalent in music.

That is why the most "musical" images in the era of silent film montage were those edited on the tonal principle, particularly landscapes almost free of movement, such as the "Mist Suite" in *Potemkin.*

Be that as it may, such is the case when the composer has to deal with finished, already edited fragments of a film.

All he has to do to obtain a complete audio-visual counterpoint is to "discover" the law underlying the structure of the fragment and include its structural formula into his musical "estimate."

It should be remembered that in editing I adhere to severe structural and compositional canons which, though at times very complex, can nevertheless be perceived quite distinctly.

The situation is somewhat different when the composer has to work with unedited material. Then he has to discover the potentialities of structural canons inherent in it.

What should not be lost sight of is the circumstance that the structure of the separate pieces shot for any scene is not accidental, that each piece in a scene (and not only in scenes with an acted theme but in purely "symphonic" ones, that is, showing lyrical landscapes, battles, where there are no protagonists, tempests, fires, hurricanes, etc.) is by no means fortuitous.

If a piece is a truly "montage" one, that is, not disconnected but meant to produce an image together with other pieces, it will, at the very moment it is shot, be infused with elements which characterize its inner essence and at the same time contain the seeds of the structure most suited for the fullest possible revelation of this essence in the finished compositional form.

And if the composer is faced with (for the time being) a chaotic agglomeration of pieces with such structural potentialities, his task will not be to discover the finished structure of the whole but to find in the individual elements the seeds of the future structure and, proceeding from these, to set down the compositional form into which the pieces will fit organically.*

How wonderfully Prokofiev adheres to the montage principle in the construction of his musical images!

It is montage that produces the sense of the three-dimensional in the cinema.

How plastically flat are the representations of men, objects, settings and landscape shot in one piece, from one angle.

And how they come to life all of a sudden, how they become rounded and acquire volume, how they become spatial as soon as you begin juxtaposing in montage their individual aspects shot from different angles.

I am tempted to say of individual shots what Benvenuto Cellini wrote in 1547 about painting and sculpture to Bendeto Varchi:

"... I affirm that sculpture is eight times greater an art than any of the other fine arts, for a statue has eight angles from which it should be viewed and from each it should be equally perfect....

"... A painting is a kind of statue presented only from one of the eight angles from which a sculpture should be viewed....

"... There are more than eight such angles. There are really more than forty of them, for if a sculpture is turned, even by an inch at a time, there will always be some muscle that either stands out too much or is not sufficiently noticeable, and for that reason a sculpture represents an inexhaustible multiplicity of aspects....

"... The difficulties in this respect are so great that there is not a single statue in the world that is equally perfect from every angle...."

So, if perfect "sculpturedness" in a statue can be achieved from at

* The "editor" does pretty much the same as he "bends his inner ear" to the potentialities of the pieces and gives a final structural shape to what the "director" visualizes while shooting. I must emphasize that I am speaking of scenes shot on the true "montage" principle, and not those that present nothing more than a series of talking long and medium shots which do not lend themselves even to the elementary method of "splicing" by overlapping the speaker and the listeners.— *Author's Note.*

least eight angles, then the juxtaposition of the eight individual aspects will naturally produce in our senses a realization of its three-dimensional nature and volume.

This realization will grow infinitely stronger if these individual aspects of an object are fixed in consecutive shots of appropriate size and duration, that is, if they are rationally and purposefully edited.

Benvenuto Cellini said elsewhere that "the difference between painting and sculpture is as great as that between an object and its shadow."

This parallel holds good as regards the difference between our perception of an object represented in volume or space, photographed on the montage principle, from many angles, or giving a general view from one.*

Just as a scene photographed from one angle is plastically "flat" and "lacking depth," so is "illustrative" music trivial and expressionless if it is presented "from one angle," that is, if it illustrates some one aspect, one element of what is present in the music.

And what a convincing "relief" musical image—of, say, an ocean, a fire, a storm, an impassable forest or majestic mountain peaks— arises in our senses when the melody is built on that same principle of unity through multiformity which underlies not only plastic relief in montage but also the complex montage image.

In this latter instance individual representative aspects are assigned to the different "parts" of the progression, to individual instruments or groups of instruments, and the harmonic or contrapuntal combination of these aspects produces an all-embracing general image of the whole.

And this image is not a flat imprint, not a "sound silhouette" seen from some particular angle, but a full, deep and rounded-out reflection of the event, re-created in all its multiformity and entirety.

... Prokofiev and I are in the orchestra.

The musicians are rehearsing one of Prokofiev's most beautiful

* I am speaking only of the plastic aspect of the perception of relief achieved through montage So much has been written about other expressive and sense functions and potentialities of montage that there is no need to go over them again here.—*Author's Note.*

songs for *Ivan the Terrible*—the "Blue, blue ocean," which speaks of the tsar's dream of finding an outlet to the sea.

Prokofiev's lanky figure moving among the swaying bows of the musicians seems to be floating among feather-grass.

He bends now over one, now over another, to check if they are playing correctly.

And all the while he converses with me in a whisper, pointing at the musicians.

I am told that "this one is playing light gliding over the waves, that one—the swelling waves, this one—vastness and that one—the mysterious depth."

Each instrument, each group of instruments presents in motion one or another aspect of the element of the ocean, and together they re-create, call to life (but not copy from life) and collectively produce a wonderful image of the vast and boundless ocean, foaming like an impatient charger, heaving stormy breakers, or lying placidly, quietly sleeping, its blueness mottled with patches of sunlight, just as the builder of the Russian state sees it in his dream.

For the blueness of the ocean is not merely the colour of the sky reflected in its depth, but the colour of the dream.

The sleeping watery depths are not merely elemental forces, quiet for a time but raising mountains of water in a storm, but the symbol of the deep feelings rising from the innermost depths of the soul of a people ready to perform miraculous exploits to realize this dream.

What we have is not a flat oleograph of the sea, not even an elemental and dynamic image of a real ocean, but a much more majestic and at the same time lyrical image of a man who cherishes a childlike dream and who is dangerous in wrath—the image of a man and the state he is leading towards the acquisition of sea borders.*

* * *

Prokofiev is a man of the screen in that special sense which makes it possible for the screen to reveal not only the appearance and substance of objects, but also, and notably, their peculiar inner structure.

---

* It is a noteworthy fact that it is exactly through the juxtaposition of its individual elements and phases of "behaviour" that Gogol creates the astonishingly vivid, elemental and dynamic image of the Dnieper in his *Terrible Revenge*.— *Author's Note*.

The logic of their existence. The dynamics of their development.

We have seen how for decades the "Leftist" painters have sought, at an incalculable cost in effort, to resolve those difficulties which the screen solves as easily as if it were a child's play. Dynamics, movement, chiaroscuro, transitions from form to form, rhythm, plastic twists, etc.

Unable to achieve such perfection, the painters have paid for their experiments with the representative quality and objectivity of the image.

The cinema is the only plastic art that has resolved all these problems of painting without loss of representation and objectivity and with complete ease. At the same time the cinema is capable of communicating much more: it alone is able to reconstruct the inner movement of phenomena profoundly and fully.

The camera angle reveals the secrets of nature.

The juxtaposition of various camera angles reveals the artist's attitude to the phenomenon.

Montage structure unites the objective existence of the phenomenon and the artist's subjective attitude to it.

None of the severe standards modern painting sets for itself is relinquished. At the same time everything preserves the full vitality of the phenomenon.

It is in this particular sense that Prokofiev's music is amazingly plastic. It is never content with remaining an illustration. Sparkling with triumphant imagery, it presents a wonderful picture of the inner movement of the phenomenon and its dynamic structure, which embody the emotion and meaning of the event.

Whether it be the march from the fantastic *Love for Three Oranges*, the duel between Mercutio and Tybalt, the gallop of the Teuton Knights in *Alexander Nevsky*, or the entrance of Kutuzov in the finale of *War and Peace*—everywhere, in the very nature of the phenomena, Prokofiev knows how to grasp the structural secret which conveys the broad meaning of the phenomenon.

Having grasped the structural secret of a phenomenon, he clothes it in the tonal camera angles of instrumentation, making it sparkle with shifts of timbre, and forces the whole inflexible structure to blossom forth in the emotional fulness of orchestration.

He throws the moving graphic outlines of his musical images on to our consciousness just as the blinding beam of the projector flings moving images on to the white surface of the screen. It is not an engraved impression of a phenomenon in painting, but a something that pierces the phenomenon by means of tonal chiaroscuro.

I am not speaking of Prokofiev's musical technique, but I see the "steel step" of *staccato* consonants beating out the clarity of thought in those places where many others would have been tempted to use indistinctly modulated nuances of vowels.

If Prokofiev were to write articles, he would dedicate them to the wise props of speech—to the consonants.

In the same way as he writes operas, leaning not on the melody of rhymes, but on the bony angularity of unrhythmic prose.

... He would write his sonnets to the consonants.

But stop—what's this?

On the dotted line of an artfully worded contract—in the cordial inscriptions on photographs presented to friends and admirers—in the upper right-hand corner of the music-sheet of a new piece—we always see the harsh tap-dance of consonants:

P—R—K—F—V

This is his usual signature!

He even spells his name with nothing but consonants!

Bach saw a divine melodic pattern in the letters of his name; the letters B-A-C-H arranged themselves in a melodic line on which he based one of his works.

The consonants with which Prokofiev signs his name could be read as a symbol of the undeviating consistency of his talent.

From the composer's creative work—as from his signature—everything unstable, transient, accidental, or capricious has been expelled.

This is how they wrote on ancient icons:

Gospod (Lord) was written *Gd*, and Tsar, *Tsr*, and *Rzhstvo Btsy* stood for Rozhdestvo Bogoroditsy (Birth of the Mother of God).

The strict spirit of the old Slavonic canon was reflected in these eliminations of everything accidental, transient, mundane.

In teaching, the canon leaned on the eternal, over the transient.

In painting—on the essential rather than on the ephemeral.

In inscriptions—on the consonants, apparently symbols of the eternal as opposed to the accidental.

This is what we find in the ascetic drum-beat of those five consonants—P, R, K, F, V—sensed through the dazzling radiation of Prokofiev's musical chiaroscuro.

It is thus that the gold letters burn dimly on the frescoes of Spaso-Nereditsa.

Or they echo the abbot's stern call through the flood of sepia and the celestial azure of cobalt in the murals of Feofan the Greek in the vaults of the Fyodor Stratilat Church in Novgorod.

Equal to the inflexible severity of Prokofiev's writing is the magnificence of his lyricism which, like Aaron's rod, blossoms in that miracle of Prokofiev's orchestration.

Prokofiev is profoundly national.

But not in the *kvass* and *shchi* manner of the conventionally Russian pseudo-realists.

Nor is he national in the sense Perov and Repin are—in detail and *genre*.

Prokofiev is national in the severely traditional sense that dates back to the primitive Scythian and the unsurpassed perfection of the thirteenth-century stone carvings in the cathedrals of Vladimir and Suzdal.

His nationalism springs from the very sources that shaped the national consciousness of the Russian people, the sources that are reflected in the old frescoes created by our wise people or in the icon craftsmanship of Rublyov.

That is why antiquity resounds so beautifully in Prokofiev's music, expressed not by archaic or stylized means, but by the most extreme and hazardous twists of ultra-modern musical idiom.

Here, we find in Prokofiev the same paradoxical synchronization we get when we juxtapose an icon with a cubist painting, Picasso with the frescoes of Spaso-Nereditsa.

Through this true (in a Hegelian sense) originality, through this "primeval nature," Prokofiev is, at the same time, both profoundly national and international.

But it is not only in this way that Prokofiev is international.

He is also international because of the protean variety of his expressive speech.

In this the canon of his musical mentality is again similar to the canons of antiquity, but in this case to the canon of Byzantine tradition, which has the faculty of shining in its own particular way in any environment.

On Italian soil it shines in the Madonnas of Cima'bue.

On Spanish soil—in the works of Domenico Theotocopuli, called El Greco.

In the former Novgorod Province—in the murals by anonymous masters, murals barbarously trampled underfoot by the invading Teuton hordes.

The art of Prokofiev, likewise, can be fired by more than purely national, historical, or patriotic themes, such as the epic events of the nineteenth, sixteenth, or thirteenth centuries (the years of *War and Peace, Ivan the Terrible,* and *Alexander Nevsky*).

The keen talent of Prokofiev, attracted by the passionate environment of Shakespeare's Renaissance Italy, flares up in a ballet based on that great dramatist's most lyrical tragedy.

In the magic environment of Gozzi's phantasmagoria,* Prokofiev produces an amazing cascade of the fantastic quintessence of Italy at the end of the eighteenth century.

In the environment of the fanatical brutality of the thirteenth century—the unforgettable image of the Teuton Knights' blunted iron wedge galloping with the same "irresistibility" as did the tank columns of their loathsome descendants.

Everywhere—search, severe, methodical. This reveals Prokofiev's kinship with the masters of the early Renaissance, when the painter was at the same time a philosopher and the sculptor a mathematician.

Everywhere freedom from the impressionistic "generality" of the brush-stroke, from the smeared colour of "blobs."

In his hands one senses not an arbitrary brush, but a responsible camera lens.

His place is not among backdrops, illusory landscapes and the "dizzy heights" of the stage. His place is amid microphones, kleig lights, celluloid spirals of film, the faultless accuracy of the meshing sprockets of synchronization, and mathematical calculations of length in film montage.

*   *   *

* Eisenstein mean Prokofiev's opera *Love for Three Oranges* on the subject of Gozzi's tale of that title.—*Ed.*

The blinding beam of the projector is switched off.
The ceiling lights of the hall are turned on.
Prokofiev wraps his scarf around his neck.
I can sleep calmly.
At exactly 11.55 a. m. tomorrow his small blue car will come through the studio gates. Five minutes later the score will lie on my desk.
On it will be the symbolic letters:
P — R — K — F — V.
Nothing ephemeral, nothing accidental.
Everything clear, exact, perfect.
That is why Prokofiev is not only one of the greatest composers of our time, but, in my opinion, also the most wonderful film composer.

1946

CHARLIE THE KID

Charlie the Kid. I think that this combination of Chaplin's name and the title of one of the most popular of his films, is worthy of being used to identify its creator; this appellation reveals his inner nature just as "Conqueror," "Cœur de Lion" and "Terrible" describe the natures of William of Normandy, of the legendary Richard and of the wise Tsar Ivan IV of Muscovy.
What is it that thrills me?
What is it I want to understand?
It is not direction.
Or methods.
Or tricks.
Or the technique of his humour.
When I think of Chaplin I want, first of all, to penetrate that strange system of thinking which perceives phenomena in such a strange way and responds to them with such strange images. I would like to penetrate that part of this system of thinking which, before it becomes an outlook of life, exists in the stage of contemplation of the environment.

In a word, I shall treat not of Chaplin's outlook but of his perception of life, which underlies all the unique and inimitable conceptions of what is known as "the Chaplin humour."

*　　*　　*

The fields of vision of the two eyes of a hare cross behind its head, so that it sees what is behind it.

Since it is fated more often to flee than to pursue, it does not complain. But its fields of vision do not cross in front; the hare does not see what is in front of it. It is apt to collide with anything.

A hare sees the world differently from us.

The sheep's eyes are set so that the fields of vision do not cross at all. A sheep sees two worlds—a right world and a left world—which do not make a visual whole.

Different ways of seeing result in different pictures and images. To say nothing of the higher processes which the things we see undergo in being transformed into the *perception of the world* and, later, the *world outlook*, when we leave hares and sheep and take up man with all the social factors around him that go to make up a world outlook.

How are his eyes set—I mean *mental* eyes, how does he look with his eyes—I mean again mental eyes?

What do his eyes see?

What do those unusual eyes—Chaplin's eyes—see?

The eyes that can see Dante's Inferno or Goya's *capriccio* of the *Modern Times* behind the forms of carefree gaiety.

And what thrills me,

what interests me,

what I want to understand—

is:

With whose eyes does Charlie Chaplin look on life?

*　　*　　*

One of Chaplin's *characteristics* is that in spite of his grey hair he has preserved a "child's outlook" on life and spontaneous perception of events.

Hence his freedom from the "fetters of morals" and his ability to see as comic things which make other people's flesh creep.

168

To. my friend Sergei Eisenstein
with my sincere admiration
Charlie Chaplin

Hollywood - Nov. 18th 30

Charlie Chaplin's autographed photo

Eisenstein and Chaplin
(Hollywood 1930)

Such a trait in an adult is known as infantilism.

Hence Chaplin's comic constructions are based chiefly on an infantile method.

This statement needs two reservations:

This method is not the only one Chaplin uses, and it is not used by Chaplin alone.

It is true that we tried less to define his methods than to solve the "secret of his eyes," the secret of his outlook from which spring all and sundry methods.

But first let us find out why, out of all the ways and means of producing the comic effect that can humanly be used, Chaplin chooses the one we have defined, thus appearing as the most representative personality in American humour.

It is precisely the *infantilism* of humour that makes him the most American of all American humorists. And not because, as it is usually asserted, the mentality of the average American is that of a fourteen-year-old child.

The word "infantilism" cannot be found in Flaubert's "List of Copy-Book Truths."

If he had entered it, he would have written as he did about Diderot: *"Diderot is always followed by d'Alembert."*

Infantilism is always followed by escape from reality.

In the present instance this is all the more true, for the impulse to escape which drove Rimbaud from Paris to Abyssinia or Gauguin to Tahiti, can drive one much farther from today's New York.

"Civilization" today fetters so wide an area that similar Ritz hotels (and not only hotels) are to be found with maddening regularity not only in any sizable town of Europe or the U.S.A. but in the most out-of-the-way spots on the Island of Bali, in Addis Ababa, in the tropics or among eternal snows.

"Geographical" escapism has been rendered ineffective by the spread of air routes. What remains is "evolutionary" escapism—a downward course in one's development, back to the ideas and emotions of "golden childhood," which may well be defined as "regress towards infantilism," escape to a personal world of childish ideas.

In a strictly-regulated society, where life follows strictly-defined canons, the urge to escape from the chains of things "established once and for all" must be felt particularly strongly.

When I think of America I invariably recollect two things: the test for a driver's licence and the story I read in a magazine published by some college or other about an examination in the humanities. In both instances—an examination.

In the former you are handed a questionnaire.

The questions are so formulated that all you have to write is "yes" or "no."

A question does not read, "What is the top speed in passing a school?" It reads, "Can you drive past a school at a speed exceeding 20 miles?"

The expected answer is "No."

"In driving along a narrow road, can you cross a highway without stopping at the cross-roads?"

The expected answer is "No."

Questions requiring a positive answer are formulated in the same way.

But you will never find a question worded as follows: "What must you do to cross a highway when driving along a narrow road?"

The person examined is never expected to think for himself or to arrive at his own *conclusions*.

Everything is reduced to *automatic memorizing*, to "Yes" or "No" answers.

The automation with which the answers are checked is also very revealing.

Over the questionnaire is placed a sheet of paper with perforations in the places where "yes" must be written.

Then another paper is put over the questionnaire, this time with perforations where "no's" are expected to be written.

The examiner looks over the one, then the other and sees at once whether the open spaces in the first instance show only positive answers and in the second—only negative ones.

You would think this was an excellent invention to standardize the issue of drivers' licences.

But....

Here is a funny story in a magazine about a college class taking their exam.

With bated breath everybody is listening to how ... a blind student is typing.

First two clicks. Then three. ...

And the whole class write hurriedly by the sound of the typewriter.
First there was a "no."
Then there was a "yes."
The familiar "driver's system" again! The same grid.
The same game of "yes" and "no."
The mechanical grid and the blind student leading those who see combine into one symbol.
The symbol of a whole mechanical and automatic intellectual system.
A kind of an intellectual assembly-line.
And it is quite natural that one longs to escape from it.
While Chaplin finds a physical way out of the tangles of machinism in his "leaping representations" in *Modern Times*, it is in the method of infantilism, providing a "leap" beyond intellectual machinism, that he finds the intellectual and emotional way out.
In doing this Chaplin shows that he is a hundred per cent American.
A philosophical system in general and the applied interpretation of its individual spheres always reflect the main nostalgia rending the heart of a people or a nation existing in definite social environment.
There is as much right to say, "You shall know them by their theories" as there is to use this saying regarding deeds.
Let us study the typically American interpretation of the secret of comedy. I warn you beforehand that all theories and explanations of the comic are local and relative. But just now we are not interested in the degree to which this interpretation of the secret of comedy is true and objective.
What we are interested in is the specifically American attitude towards the problem of the comic, just as we consider interesting the interpretations offered by Kant and Bergson primarily as individual and social "documents of their times," and not as universal truths about the theory of the ridiculous embracing ridiculously little of the phenomenon.
To suit our purpose, therefore, we shall look for a typically American theoretic *source* expounding the fundamentals of the comic.
If we were looking for a typically German source we would turn to the metaphysicists; for a typically British source we would apply to the Essayists who, through their spokesman, Meredith, have proclaimed humour the privilege of the select minds. And so on and so forth.

But since we want to study the typically American approach and the typically American understanding of humour, we shall not turn to the metaphysicists, or to the satirists, or to the philosophers or Essayists.

We shall turn to the practics.

American pragmatism in philosophy is a reflection of this avid search for what is *useful and applicable*—in everything that interests the American.

Hence countless books on methods of "conditioning people by means of humour."

I have read dozens of pages on how to use wit to arouse interest in a report or a sermon; on how to use humour to get more during a collection in church; on how travelling salesmen use witty jokes to get people to buy the vacuum cleaners or washing-machines they do not need.

The recipes offered are tight, unerring and highly effective.

All is reduced to flattery in some form or other, or even to common bribery.

Sometimes the recipes are supplied with brief theoretical introductions.

I shall quote just from one such book which offers probably the most "perfectly American" understanding of the appeal of humour.

And we shall see that the most "perfectly American" (although enjoying world fame) comic lends himself fully to this explanation.

I shall not be sparing of quotations. Their content apart, the very fact that such books are published, is graphic evidence that "Americanism" engenders a reaction in the shape of those peculiar methods of comedy which facilitate escape just from this same "Americanism."

This book was written in 1925 by Professor H. A. Overstreet, Head of the Department of Philosophy, College of the City of New York. It is called *Influencing Human Behavior* and is a symposium of lectures delivered on the request of a group of his students.

The author himself remarks in the foreword that the request was "unusual" and "significant."

It came as a petition "for a course indicating how human behaviour can actually be changed in the light of the new knowledge gained through psychology.... We have in common an interest in understanding and improving social conditions. Besides this, and perhaps first of all, we desire to utilize as a part of our everyday technique of action such knowledge as modern psychology can furnish us. Our interest is not academic. We wish actually to function with such knowledge as we may gain."

In his preface, the practical psychologist gave an answer in keeping with the technical nature of the request.

"The object of these chapters is to discover how far the data of modern psychology can be put to use by each of us in furthering what is really the central concern of our lives. That central concern is the same whether we be teachers, writers, parents, merchants, statesmen, preachers, or any other of the thousand and one types into which civilization has divided us. In each case the same essential problem confronts us.... What is this central problem? Obviously, it is to be, in some worthwhile manner, effective within our human environment.

"We are writers? Then there is the world of editors, some of whom we must convince as to our ability. If we succeeded in doing that, then there is, further, the reading public. It is a bit of sentimental nonsense to say that it makes no difference at all if a writer convinces not even a single soul of his pertinence and value, so be it only that he 'express' himself. We have a way of being overgenerous with so-called misunderstood geniuses. True, this is a barbarian world; and the fine soul has its hard innings.... At any rate, as his manuscripts come back, he might well cease putting the blame on philistine editors and public long enough to ask himself whether, indeed, he is not deficient in the very elementary art of making the good things he has to say really understandable.

"We are businessmen? Then there are the thousands of potential customers whom we must induce to buy our product. If they refuse, then bankruptcy....

"We are parents? It may seem somewhat far-fetched to say that the chief concern of a parent is to be accepted by his children. 'What!' we cry, 'aren't they *our* children; and aren't children required to respect their parents?' That, of course, is all old philosophy; old ethics; old psychology as well, coming from the day when children, like wives, were our property. Nowadays children are persons; and the task of parents is to be real persons themselves to such an extent that their children accept them as of convincing power in their lives....

"We need not specify further. As individuals, our chief task in life is to make our personality, and what our personality has to offer, effective in our particular environment of human beings. . . .

"Life is many things; it is food-getting, shelter-getting, playing, fighting, aspiring, hoping, sorrowing. But at the centre of it all it is this: it is the process of getting ourselves believed in and accepted. . . .

"How are we to become intelligent about this?. . .

"Not by talking vaguely about goals and ideals; but by finding out quite specifically what methods are to be employed if the individual is to 'get across' to his human fellows, is to capture their attention and win their regard, is to induce them to think and act along with him—whether his human fellows be customers or clients or pupils or children or wife; and whether the regard which he wishes to win is for his goods, or ideas, or artistry, or a great human cause. . . .

"To become skilled artists in the enterprise of life—there is hardly anything more basically needful than this. It is to this problem that we address ourselves."

I was at great pains not to put several exclamation marks after each "gem" of this apology of practicism which puts a writer, a businessman and a parent in the same category, and speaks in one breath about a customer and a wife, goods and ideas.

But let us proceed in perusing Professor Overstreet's guide in which some passages rival the finest pages written by Labiche and Scribe.

Here is a division entitled "Yes-Response Technique."

"The canvasser rings the doorbell.

"The door is opened by a suspicious lady-of-the-house.

"The canvasser lifts his hat. 'Would you buy an illustrated *History of the World*?' he asks.

" 'No!'

"And the door slams.

"In the above there is a psychological lesson.

"A 'No' response is a most difficult handicap to overcome. If a person has said 'No' all his pride of personality demands that he remain consistent with himself.

"He may later feel that the 'No' was ill-advised, nevertheless, there is his precious pride to consider! Once having said a thing, he must stick to it.

"Hence it is of the very greatest importance that we start a person in the affirmative direction.

"A wiser canvasser rings the doorbell.

"An equally suspicious lady-of-the-house opens.

"The canvasser lifts his hat.

" 'This is Mrs. Armstrong?'

"Scowlingly—'Yes.'

" 'I understand, Mrs. Armstrong, that you have several children in school?'

"Suspiciously—'Yes.'

" 'And of course they have much homework to do?'

"Almost with a sigh—'Yes.'

" 'That always requires a good deal of work with reference books, doesn't it—hunting things up, and so on? And of course we don't want our children running out to the library every night . . . better for them to have all these materials at home.' Etc., etc.

"We do not guarantee the sale. But that second canvasser is destined to go far! He has captured the secret of getting, at the outset a number of 'yes-responses.' He has thereby set the psychological process of his listener moving in the affirmative direction. . . ."

*　*　*

On page 257 of this "guide" you find a business-like presentation of the key, not to the abstract understanding of humour in general, but to the American understanding of its secrets, or rather, to that understanding of the nature of humour which is the most effective as applied to the American.

Professor Overstreet begins with the correct observation that "it is almost the greatest reproach to tell a person flatly that he has no sense of humour." Tell him that he is disorderly, or lackadaisical, or homely, or awkward; he will bear up under these. But tell him that he has no sense of humour; it is a blow from which even the best of us find it difficult to recover.

" . . . People have a most curious sensitiveness in this regard."

I can confirm the correctness of this observation by citing as example the most perfect of all exponents of humour, Chaplin himself.

There is nothing further from my intention than to write a theoretical treatise, so I snatch at every pretext to substitute personal recollections for speculations.

A night in Beverly Hills, Hollywood.

We were entertaining Chaplin.

We were playing a very popular Hollywood game.

A cruel game.

It is very typical of a spot where on an area of a few square miles are concentrated so many self-esteems, self-loves and self-infatuations, deserved and undeserved, well-founded and wholly unfounded, overestimated and underestimated, but in all cases so painfully alert that they would have sufficed for three-quarters of the globe's population.

The game is a variation of the popular "game of opinions."

With that difference that here you express your opinion by means of putting down "marks" in a questionnaire, for instance, *cleverness* 5, *wit* 3, *glamour* 4, etc.

The one who is discussed must fill in a similar questionnaire, in accordance with his own opinion of himself.

"Self-criticism game," is what it would be called in Moscow.

The more so that its effect lies not in guesses but in the degree to which public opinion of you differs from your own.

A cruel game!

And especially because the *sense of humour* column occupies a prominent place in it.

The King of Humour quietly went to the kitchen and, donning his spectacles, filled in his questionnaire somewhere near the refrigerator.

Meanwhile a surprise was in store for him:

Public opinion had rated the King of Humour's sense of humour ... at 4.

Did he grasp the humour of the situation?

He did not!

He was offended.

The illustrious visitor lacked the sense of humour when it touched himself. So the *4* was well deserved after all!

Professor Overstreet goes on to ask why people are so upset when they see others doubt their sense of humour?

"Apparently," he answers, "the possession of humour implies the possession of a number of typical habit-systems. The first is an emotional one: the habit of playfulness. Why should one be proud of being playful? For a double reason. First, playfulness connotes childhood and youth. If one can be playful, one still possesses something of the vigour and the joy of young life. If one has ceased to be playful, one writes oneself as rigidly old. And who wishes to confess to himself that, rheumatic as are his joints, his mind and spirit are really aged? So the old man is proud of the playful joke which assures him that he is still friskily young.

"But there is a deeper implication. To be playful is, in a sense, to be free. When a person is playful, he momentarily disregards the binding necessities which compel him, in business and morals, in domestic and community life. . . .

". . . Life is largely compulsion. But in play we are free! We do what we please. . . .

"Apparently there is no dearer human wish than to be free.

"But this is not simply a wish to be free *from*; it is also, and more deeply, a wish to be free *to*. What galls us is that the binding necessities do not permit us to shape our world as we please. . . . What we most deeply desire, however, is to create our world for ourselves. Whenever we can do that, even in the slightest degree, we are happy. Now in play we create our own world. . . .

"To imply, therefore, that a person has a fine sense of humour is to imply that he has still in him the spirit of play, which implies even more deeply the spirit of freedom and of creative spontaneity."

The subsequent practical recipes are based wholly on these premises.

For the specifically American state of humour Prof. Overstreet's speculations are extremely apt, they are quite correctly derived from the fundamentals of American psychology.

Legions of American comedians follow the road he has charted.

And the most perfect of them does this with utmost perfection, for he serves this principle not only through infantilism, gags and tricks as such, but through the subtlety of his method which, offering the spectator an infantile pattern to be imitated, psychologically infects him with infantilism and draws him into the "golden age" of the infantile paradise of childhood.

For Chaplin himself the leap into infantilism is a means of psychological escape from the limits of the regulated, ruled and calculated world around him. That isn't much. . . . A mere palliative. . . . But that is what he with his abilities can do.

In his longing for freedom Chaplin defines the artist's only means of complete escape from all restrictions through his art in a statement about... animated cartoons. Animated cartoons, he said then, were the only true art because it was in them and only in them that the artist was absolutely free and that his fantasy could do what he liked.

That was certainly a groan.

A groan expressing the longing to escape fully and completely from the conventionalities and necessities of reality which Prof. Overstreet has so obligingly enumerated in the foregoing passages.

Chaplin partially satisfies this nostalgia for freedom in the psychological "plunge" into the "golden age" of infantilism.

His spectators, whom he takes with him on his magic journey into the world of fiction and carefree and undisturbed existence which they knew only in the cradle, also find satisfaction in what he shows them.

The business-like formality of America can in many respects be considered an offspring of the primness of Dickens' Dombey. Little wonder, then, that in England, too, there was that inevitable "infantile" reaction. It found expression first of all in the subjects and plots of literary works: it was in England that the child was first introduced into novels and it was there that whole novels or large parts of novels fully devoted to child psychology made their first appearance. In novels Mr. Dombey is *Dombey and S o n*, a great deal of space is given to little Paul, David Copperfield, Little Dorrit, Nicholas Nickleby, to list the works of the most popular British author alone.

On the other hand, it was England, too, where infantilism in literature known as *nonsense* flourished with exceptional profusion. The best specimens of this style are Lewis Carroll's immortal *Alice* and Edward Lear's *The Book of Nonsense*, although Swinburne, Dante Gabriel Rossetti and even John Ruskin have left us amusing works of poetical nonsense in the form of limericks.

"Escape from reality."

"Relapse to childhood."

"Infantilism."

In the Soviet Union we are not fond of these words. We don't like the notions they express. And we have no sympathy with them.

Why?

Because the Soviet state has brought us in practice to a different solution of the problem of freeing man and the human spirit.

At the opposite end of the world people have no alternative but to flee, psychologically and fictitiously, back to the enchanting, carefree world of childhood.

At our end of the world we do not escape from reality to fairy-tale; we make fairy-tales real.

Our task is not to plunge adults into childhood but to make the children's paradise of the past accessible to every grown-up, to every citizen of the Soviet Union.

For, whatever article of the Constitution we may take, we see the state-legalized and logically presented traits of the things that go to make up an ideal golden age.

"The right to work."

What startling revelations this seemingly paradoxical formula about work brought in its time to those who invariably considered work an onerous burden, an unpleasant necessity.

How new and unexpectedly beautiful the word "work" sounded in association with the words "honour," "glory" and "heroism"!

And yet this thesis, reflecting the real state of things in our country where there is no unemployment and where every citizen is guaranteed work, is *psychologically* a wonderful revival—in a new and more perfect stage of mankind's evolution—of that premise which *in the infancy* of humanity, in that golden age, seemed to man in his primordial, natural and simple condition to be the natural conception of labour and the rights and obligations it involves.

For the first time in our country everyone is free to engage in any creative endeavour he or she may wish.

He does not have to be an aristocrat to become a diplomat.

A future statesman need not be entered the day he is born in a privileged school, outside of which there is no hope of his ever pursuing a political career.

No caste or estate privileges are necessary for a man to occupy a commanding post in the army.

And so on. . . .

There has never been such a state of affairs in any other society.

That is why the dream obsessing humanity since the dawn of history, the dream of being and doing all, could only find an outlet in hopes, myths, legends and songs.

*   *   *

179

Our record of achievement is still greater: the wise measures providing for old age have removed one more heavy burden from the Soviet man—the burden of constant anxiety about the future, the burden of feelings unknown to animals, birds, flowers and little children who are absolutely free from all care.

From the Soviet man has been removed the burden of anxiety about the much-vaunted security under which every American is staggering regardless of his material position and place on the social ladder.

That is why Chaplin's genius was born and developed at the other end of the world and not in a country where everything has been done to make the golden paradise of childhood a reality.

That is why his genius was bound to shine in a country where the method and type of his humour was a necessity, where the realization of a childish dream by a grown-up man comes against insurmountable obstacles.

* * *

Modern Times has undoubtedly revealed the "secret of his eyes." So long as his splendid comedies dealt with conflicts between good and bad people, small and big, who, as if by accident, were at the same time divided into the rich and poor, his eyes laughed or cried, depending on his theme. But when in the years of American depression the good and bad personages suddenly turned out to be real representatives of the antagonist social groups, Chaplin's eyes began to blink, then closed, and then stubbornly fixed themselves on the modern times and *new* phenomena, regarding them *in the old way*, and in this he began to contradict his theme.

This made the style of his films uneven, led to the monstrous and revolting treatment of the theme, and completely revealed the secret of Chaplin's eyes.

What I am going to say further is not meant to represent Chaplin as wholly indifferent to the environment or as not understanding (albeit in part) what takes place around him. I am not interested in what he understands. I am interested in how he perceives. How he looks and sees when he is in the grip of inspiration, when he sees before him a series of images of the events he is laughing at and when the things perceived through laughter are shaped into comic situations and tricks. I am interested to know with what eyes must one look at the world to see it as it seems to Chaplin.

A group of charming Chinese children are laughing gaily.

The group is presented in "different shots." Close-up. Medium shot. Again close-up.

What are they laughing at?

Perhaps at what is taking place deep in the room.

What is it they see?

A man (probably drunk) lies sprawling on the bed. A small Chinese woman furiously slaps his face. The children roar with laughter.

Although the man is their own father. And the little woman their mother. And the big man is not drunk. And the little woman is not slapping her husband because he is drunk.

The man is dead.

She is beating the dead man for dying and deserting her and the little children who are now laughing merrily but who will have nothing to eat.

This is not from a Chaplin film.

This is a passage from *La condition humaine* by André Malraux.

Whenever I think of Chaplin I always see him as a little Chinese boy laughing merrily at the sight of the grotesquely wobbling head of the big man as the little woman slaps him.

It little concerns him that the woman is his mother and the man his jobless father. And it concerns him least of all that the man is—dead.

Here lies the mystery of Chaplin, the secret of his eyes.

Here he is inimitable. Here he is great.

... To be able to see the most terrible, the most pitiful, the most tragic things through the eyes of a laughing child.

To be able to perceive the image of these things spontaneously and quickly—without their moral and ethical interpretation, without speculating or passing his judgement on them, just as a laughing child sees them—that is what distinguishes Chaplin, makes him unique and inimitable.

The spontaneousness of seeing engenders the perception of the ridiculous and the perception overgrows into a conception.

The conception has three aspects.

The event is quite harmless—and Chaplin's perception clothes it in inimitable buffoonery.

The event is dramatic in a personal way—and Chaplin's perception gives rise to a humorous melodrama of the best specimens of his individual style in which smiles are mixed with tears.

A blind girl makes one smile as she pours water over Chaplin, quite unconscious of his presence.

A girl whose eyesight has been restored may seem melodramatic when, touching him with her hand, she does not guess that he is the man who loves her and who has made her see.

And in that same film the melodramatic episode with the blind girl is turned topsy-turvy in the episodes with the *"bon vivant"* whom Chaplin saves from suicide; in these episodes the *"bon vivant"* recognizes his saviour only when he is "blindly" drunk.

The event is tragic in a social way. It is no longer a child's toy, no longer a problem for a child's mind, and the humorously childish look gives rise to a series of horrible shots in *Modern Times*.

A drunk encountering unemployed burglars in the shop....

The scene with the red flag....

The episode of unintentional provocation at the gate of a factory on strike....

The mutiny in the prison....

Chaplin's look makes one see things as "funny."

This finds its realization in the ethical tendency of *The Kid* and of *City Lights*, in the sentimental Christmas-Eve settings of *The Gold Rush* and in the exposure of *Dog's Life*.

It is perfectly good in *The Pilgrim*, it is magnificent in *City Lights* and entirely out of place in *Modern Times*.

What strikes one most is this ability to see spontaneously with a child's eyes, to see things *as they are*, without moral and ethical interpretation or understanding.

Application and use.

Elaboration and arrangement—conscious or unconscious, closely connected with or separable from the initial impulse.

Purposeful or unrelated.

Simultaneous or consecutive.

But all this is secondary, available, understandable, attainable, professional, a matter of craftsmanship peculiar to the entire comic epic of the American film.

But the ability to see *with a child's eyes* is the inimitable, the unique trait which Chaplin alone possesses.

Only Chaplin can see things in this light.

And through all the contrivances of professional elaboration there peers the sharp Chaplin eye, his most astonishing characteristic.

It is present always and everywhere, from a trifle like *A Night in the Show* to the tragedy of our days in *Modern Times*.

* * *

Only a genius can see the world in this light and have the courage to present it so on the screen.

Come to think of it, he does not need courage.

Because this is the only way he can see things.

Perhaps I insist on this premise too forcefully?

Perhaps!

We are men with conscious tasks.

We are all of us "grown-ups."

We are grown-ups and have lost the ability to laugh at funny things without paying attention to their possibly tragic meaning and content.

We are grown-ups, past the "irresponsible" age of childhood, free of ethics, morals, the higher criterion, etc., etc.

Reality itself brings grist to Chaplin's mill.

Chaplin sees war as a bloody incongruity in *Shoulder Arms*.

He sees the new era of our day in *Modern Times*.

It is not true that Chaplin's partner is a terrible-looking, tall, strong and ruthless fat man who runs a Hollywood restaurant when he is free from his work at the studios.

In all his repertoire Chaplin has another partner, still taller, still more terrible, still stronger and still more ruthless. With this partner —reality—Chaplin performs an endless series of circus stunts for us. Reality is like a grim "white-faced clown." It seems wise and logical, prudent and far-seeing. But in the end it is fooled, ridiculed. Its guileless and childlike partner, Chaplin, gains the upper hand. He laughs in a carefree manner, without realizing that his laughter is a verdict on reality.

Like a student in chemistry who, having been deliberately given water for his first analysis, finds every possible and impossible substance in it, so can anyone else find anything he wants in this pure water of the infantile and spontaneous perception of the comic.

As a child I once saw a magician. He walked up and down the darkened stage like a dim phosphorescent ghost.

"Keep thinking of the one you want to see!" that side-show Cagliostro shouted. "Think of him and you'll see him!"

And in the little gay man, in this wizard and magician, people see what he never means to show them.

A night in Hollywood. Charlie and I are going to Santa Monica, to the Venice festival on the beach. In a few moments we'll shoot at mechanical pigs and throw balls at apples and bottles.

Putting on his spectacles in a business-like way, Charlie will mark down the score in order to get one big prize, say an alarm-clock, instead of several small prizes like the plaster of Paris statuette of Felix the Cat. The boys will slap him on the back with a familiar "Hello, Charlie!"

As we get into the car he hands me a small book. In German. "Please tell me what it's all about." He doesn't know German. But he knows that the book is about him.

"Please tell me what it's all about."

The book is by a German impressionist, a play dealing of course with cosmic cataclysm, and in the finale Charlie Chaplin pierces revived chaos with his stick, showing the way beyond the world, and takes off his bowler in a parting bow.

I must admit I got stuck in interpreting this post-war stuff.

"Please tell me what it's all about."

Chaplin might say this of many a thing written about him.

It is astonishing, the way all kind of metaphysical nonsense springs up around Chaplin!

I recall one more thing said about Chaplin.

This was by the late Elie Faure, the author of a voluminous history of arts.

"He shifts his feet—those sad and ridiculous feet—and thereby represents the two extremes in thinking—knowledge and desire. By shifting his feet he strives for psychic balance, which he finds only to lose it immediately again."

Irrespective of his will, the social fate of his environment suggests an unerring interpretation of his works.

However it may be, Truth in the West chooses this little man with the ability to see the comic in order to put in his way, under the guise of the ridiculous, things which often are beyond that category.

Yes, Chaplin's partner is reality.

What a satirist must introduce into his works on two planes, Chaplin the comedian presents on one plane. He laughs spontaneously. Satirical interpretation is achieved by the fade-in of Chaplin's grimace on the conditions that have given rise to it.

* * *

"You remember the scene in *Easy Street* where I scatter food from a box to poor children as if they were chickens?"

This conversation took place aboard Chaplin's yacht when we spent three days off Catalina Island, in the company of sea lions, flying fish rising from the "gardens" under water, which you could watch through the glass bottom of special little steamers.

"You see, I did this because I despise them. I don't like children."

The author of *The Kid*, which had made five-sixths of the globe shed tears over the fate of the neglected child, did not like children. So he was a monster!?

But who *normally* does not like children?

Why, the children themselves.

The yacht was steaming on its way. Its rocking reminded Charlie of the way one is rocked riding an elephant.

"I despise elephants. To be so strong and so submissive!"

"What animal do you like?"

"The wolf," came the unhesitating answer. His grey eyes, the grey bristles of his eyebrows and hair lent him a wolf-like appearance. His eyes were resting on the rays of the setting sun on the Pacific waves. A U.S. destroyer was gliding over them.

A wolf.

Which is obliged to live in a pack. And is always lonely. How much like Chaplin! And always warring with his pack. Everyone an enemy to everyone else and to all.

185

Perhaps Chaplin thought a bit differently. Perhaps that was something of a pose?

But if so, it must be that pose in which Chaplin's inimitable and unique conceptions visit him.

Six months later, on the day I was leaving for Mexico, Chaplin showed me *City Lights*, roughly edited and silent.

I was sitting in Chaplin's black oilcloth arm-chair. He himself was busy supplying the sound by his own voice and piano-playing. On the screen Charlie saves a drunken rich man from drowning himself. The would-be suicide recognizes him only when drunk.

Is it funny? No, it's tragic.

It is like Shchedrin. Like Dostoyevsky. A big man is beating a little one. The little one is beaten first by a man, then by society. From one policeman in *A Dog's Life* to a regular avalanche of policemen in *Modern Times*. From carefree gaiety of *A Night in the Show* to the horrors of *Modern Times*.

The assembly-line in the film is nothing but an endless rack, mechanized Golgotha with Chaplin dancing a minuet on it.

Your flesh creeps at the sight of the handle, one turn of which changes the speed of the assembly-line.

And in the film we have paroxysms of laughter evoked by manipulations with the handle.

Long, long ago a photograph from the London *Graphic* (or was it *Sketch*?) enjoyed an immense popularity.

The caption ran: "Stop! His Majesty the Child!"

The photograph showed a stream of vehicles in Bond Street, or the Strand or Piccadilly Circus, stopped short by a bobby's hand to let a child cross the street. The traffic obediently waits for His Majesty the Child to reach the other side.

"Stop! His Majesty the Child!" I am tempted to tell myself when I try to approach Chaplin from the social-ethical and moral positions in the broad sense of these words.

"Stop!"

Let us take His Majesty as we find him!

* * *

The Chaplin situations are just what children like reading about in fairy-tales with their tortures, murders and horrors.

The favourite heroes are the frightful Ogre ("he eats little children"); Carroll's Jabberwock; the Witch.

But it takes long to read a fairy-tale. So their essence is distilled in rhymes.

The preface of *Ruthless Rhymes for Heartless Homes* by Harry Graham is as follows:

> *With guilty, conscience-stricken tears*
> *I offer up these rhymes of mine*
> *To children of maturer years*
> *(From seventeen to ninety-nine).*
> *A special solace may they be*
> *In days of second infancy.*

The rhymes addressed to those who are "in days of second infancy" preserve all that is dear to the first infancy.

THE STERN PARENT

> *Father heard his Children scream,*
> *So he threw them in the stream,*
> *Saying, as he drowned the third,*
> *"Children should be seen, not heard!"*

MR. JONES

> *"There's been an accident!" they said,*
> *"Your servant's cut in half; he's dead!"*
> *"Indeed!" said Mr. Jones, "and please,*
> *Send me the half that's got my keys."*

NECESSITY

> *Late last night I slew my wife,*
> *Stretched her on the parquet flooring;*
> *I was loth to take her life,*
> *But I had to stop her snoring.*

A dissertation could be written on the Anglo-Saxon humour as opposed to the "Slav soul" if, in connection with the last given rhyme, we recall Chekhov's dramatic treatment of the same subject in *So Sleepy*. In that story the nurse, herself little more than a child, strangles the baby in her care because it cries at night and prevents her from sleeping. The deed is done in the warm quiet light of the green icon-lamp.

All such and similar examples—the dramatic sketch of the little nurse, the fantastic occurrences in Grimm Brothers' tales, as well as the carelessly ironical *Ruthless Rhymes*—have grasped the essential in child psychology, that essential which Lev Tolstoi had noticed long ago.

This is how Maxim Gorky quotes him:

"Andersen was a lonely man. Very lonely. I do not know much about him: I believe he led a dissipated life, but this can only strengthen my conviction that he was lonely. That is why he addressed himself to children, although it is a mistaken notion that children have more sympathy with one than does a grown-up. Children do not pity anything, they know no pity."

Students of child psychology are of the same opinion.

And the curious fact is that it is precisely this that lies at the bottom of children's jokes and stories.

Yelena Kononenko has put down what she heard Moscow children say:

" 'I say, Grandad, will you see New Moscow? D'you think you'll live that long?' was Vladilen's cruel question to his grandfather. I saw that he felt somewhat uncomfortable after asking this question, his heart telling him that he had been wrong in speaking like this. It was clear that he was a bit ashamed and felt somewhat sorry for his grandfather. As a matter of fact he was not sorry for old men and when his friend told him that old men would be made into glue he laughed until tears stood in his eyes, and then slily asked me how much glue Grandad would yield."

C. W. Kimmins writes about British and American children. He uses a vast amount of statistical data. In the chapter dealing with what causes little children to laugh he says that other people's misfortunes often form the basis of funny stories. In the age group of seven-year-olds such stories are enjoyed by 25 per cent of boys and about 16 per cent of girls. In the age group of eight the percentage decreases to 18 and 10 respectively. Beginning with the age of nine and ten years, the decrease in the percentage is still more marked.

But this concerns only *stories*. The description of such *events* continues to provoke laughter in older children as well, and they are especially popular with children in the period of rapid growth, between the ages of twelve and fourteen.

In his *Child's Attitude to Life* Kimmins quotes the following story popular with the children of this age: "A man was shaving when a sudden knock was heard at the door; this startled him and he had the misfortune to cut off his nose. In his excitement he dropped his razor, which cut off one of his toes. A doctor was called in and bound up the wounds. After some days the bandages were removed, when it was found that the nose had been fixed on to the foot and the toe on to the face. The man made a complete recovery, but it was very awkward, because every time he wanted to blow his nose he had to take his boot off."

This situation is in perfect keeping with the pantomime of the English Pierrot (and of the English only) which so struck Baudelaire accustomed to the French Deburau.

He said that there was exaggeration beyond all understanding. Pierrot was passing a woman scrubbing her doorstep. He emptied her pockets and tried to steal her sponge, the broom, the soap and even the water in the bucket.

It would be hard to say for which of his crimes Pierrot was to be guillotined. And why guillotined and not hanged—in England? It is hard to say why, unless it was needed for what was to follow.

Pierrot cried out, like a cow with the smell of the abattoir in its nostrils but at last the sentence was executed. His head fell off his body—an enormous white and red head—and rolled clattering across the stage, showing the red disc of the cut throat, the broken vertebrae and other details of a carcass just prepared for sale. All of a sudden the beheaded torso moved by the spirit of acquisitiveness stood upright, picked up its own head and, displaying much more practical sense than the great St. Denis, put it into its trousers pocket as if it were a ham or a bottle of wine.

To complete the picture, we might add a story by Ambrose Bierce whose cruel "humoresques" are quite appropriate here, as they are highly characteristic of the British and American brand of humour and are rooted in the same common soil.

MAN AND GOOSE

A Man was plucking a live Goose;
When the bird addressed him thus:
"Suppose that you were a goose;
do you think that you would
relish this sort of thing?"
"Suppose that I were," said the
Man; "do you think that you
would like to pluck me?"
"Indeed I should!" was the natural,
emphatic, but injudicious reply.
"Just so," concluded her tormentor,
pulling out another handful of feathers;
"that is the way that I feel about it."

The gags in *Modern Times* are in exactly the same vein.

Wise Vassa Zheleznova in Gorky's play says, "Only children are happy and even then not for long."

Not for long, because the harsh "must nots" of their elders and of the future standards of behaviour curb the impetuous desires of children from the first steps they make.

He who does not reconcile himself with these fetters and fails to make them serve him, he who, having become a man in years, remains a child, is invariably unfit for life, finds himself in awkward situations and is ridiculous and ridiculed.

Whereas Chaplin's eye of a child decides on the choice of themes and their treatment, their plot usually evolves around comic situations showing conflicts between a child's naïve approach to life and its harsh "grown-up" reaction.

Chaplin of the back streets of the East Side has proved to be the true "Christ's simple man" of whom Wagner dreamed in his old age; Chaplin, and not Parsifal facing the Holy Grail among the luxuries of Bayreuth.

As seen by Chaplin and presented in the character of his comedies, the amoral cruelty of the child's attitude to life is concealed by the other appealing traits of childhood. By those traits which, like Paradise, have been lost by adults for ever.

Therein lies the secret of Chaplin's touching scenes which almost always escape appearing unnaturally sentimental.

Sometimes this touching quality reaches the heights of pathos.* There is something sublime in the finale of *The Pilgrim* where the impatient sheriff kicks Chaplin in the pants for failing to understand that he wanted Charlie, the escaped convict, to cross into Mexico.

In seeing the generosity of the escaped convict who pretended to be a preacher but recovered the funds of a small church, the sheriff wants to display similar generosity.

So, while escorting Chaplin along the Mexican border beyond which his prisoner will find freedom, the sheriff does his best to make Chaplin avail himself of the opportunity to escape.

Chaplin does not understand what is required of him.

Losing patience, the sheriff orders him to pick a flower on the other side of the border.

Chaplin obediently crosses the ditch beyond which lies freedom.

The sheriff, satisfied with his ruse, rides on.

But Chaplin in his childlike honesty overtakes him with the flower.

A kick in the pants cuts the dramatic knot.

Chaplin *is* free.

And then comes the best of his finales—Chaplin shambling away from the camera into the diaphragm along the border line, with one foot in the U.S.A. and the other in Mexico.

It is a common rule that the most impressive detail, episode or scene in a film is the one which, all else notwithstanding, symbolizes its author's method, is the product of the author's personality.

This is just what we have here.

One foot is on the territory of the sheriff, the law, the fetters; the other on a territory which brings him freedom from the law, from responsibility, from the court and the police.

The last shot in *The Pilgrim* may be considered a cross-section of the hero's character, the all-pervading scheme of all the conflicts in Chaplin's films, which can be reduced to one thing—a graphic repre-

---

* Here, as everywhere, the word is used in its original sense.—*Tr.*

sentation of the method by which Chaplin produces his wonderful results.

The escape into the diaphragm is almost a symbol of the hopelessness in which a semi-child finds himself in a society of fully grown people.

Let's stop here!

Let the phantom of Elie Faure serve us as a warning not to put more metaphysical meaning than is needed into the shuffle of Chaplin's feet.

All the more so that we interpret this drama in a broader sense, as the drama of "the little man" in the conditions of modern society.

Hans Fallada's *Little Man, What Now?* is like a bridge between the two interpretations.

Whatever the interpretation Chaplin himself puts in his finale, in modern society there is no way out for the little man.

Just as a child cannot remain little for ever.

Sad though it may be, he loses the attractive qualities of childhood one by one:

first *naïveté*,

then credulity,

then light-heartedness....

Just as one loses the qualities that are unacceptable in modern society:

first the unwillingness to reckon with one's neighbour,

then the unwillingness to abide by the rules of accepted behaviour,

then the spontaneous childish egoism....

Laughingly, we bid good-bye to our past.

Yes, laughingly and sorrowfully.

But then let us imagine for a moment an adult who has preserved intact the whole complex of irrepressible infantile features.

And the first and most important of these—supreme egoism and absolute freedom from "the fetters of morality."

In that case we have a brazen aggressor, Attila the conqueror. And Chaplin, who has just stigmatized the Attila of today—Hitler, once yearned to play ... Napoleon.

For a long time he was obsessed with the idea and elaborated plans for such a film.

Here is how he visualized the screen play: Napoleon on St. Helena.

He becomes a pacifist and secretly returns to France. But then he can't resist the temptation to overthrow the government.

Just as the plot is about to be realized news comes from St. Helena that Napoleon has died. You will recollect that he had a double on the island. Everybody thinks it is the "real" Napoleon who has died. His plans fall through and he dies of a broken heart. His last words are: "The news of my death has killed me."

These lines are even better than Mark Twain's famous telegram: "The news of my death is somewhat exaggerated."

Chaplin visualized the film as a tragedy.

The film was conceived but never made.

Yet the treatment is clear. Napoleon is unrecognized and wronged on his return. And tragically broken-down in the end:

"The news of my death has killed me!"

Very characteristic, that!

Irrepressible and impetuous infantilism is shackled in normal society.

On reaching a certain age His Majesty the Child is subjected to severe restraint.

In Chaplin's hands the restrained Napoleon could have become a second chained Prometheus of infantile dreams.

In the gallery of Chaplin's images Napoleon would have become the symbol of the broken ideal of infantilism.

A noticeable change is taking place in Chaplin's work under the influence of the ultra-modern times of fascism which have succeeded the era of Modern Times.

It was quite natural for Chaplin to create *The Dictator.*

Chaplin had to immortalize the raving maniac who became the head of a blinded state, of a country out of its wits.

An infantile maniac at the head of a state.

In this film Chaplin's "infantile method" of looking at life and making comedies became the salient feature of the character of a live man (if the prototype of Adenoid Hynkel *can* be called a man) and of the actual methods of governing a real country.

Chaplin's method of producing comic effects, which always triumphed over the means of his infantile approach to phenomena, was transplanted into the characterization of the protagonist in *The Dictator.*

Not curbed and restrained as before, but irrepressible, triumphant and impetuous.

The author's method determined the features of a character. And one played on the screen by the author himself.

You see this "infantile" character in full power.

Hynkel is shown studying the inventions of unsuccessful inventors.

Here is a "bullet-proof" jacket.

Hynkel's bullet goes through it.

The inventor is killed on the spot and falls like a rotten tree.

Here is a man with a funny hat-parachute jumping down from the palace roof.

The Dictator listens attentively.

Looks down.

The inventor breaks his neck.

And then follows his wonderful line: "Again you're palming off rubbish on me!"

Isn't this like a scene in the nursery?!

Characterized by the infantile freedom from morals which astonishes us so in Chaplin's way of seeing things. Freedom from the fetters of morality which enables him to ridicule any event becomes here a feature of his hero's character; an infantile trait found in a grown-up man is horrible when it typifies Hitler reality and devastatingly satirical when it is found in a parody on Hitler—in Hynkel.

Formerly Chaplin always played suffering men, like the Ghetto barber, his second role in *The Dictator*.

The Hynkels of his other films were, first, a policeman, then the giant partner who thought he was a chicken and wanted to eat him in *The Gold Rush*, then countless policemen, then the assembly-line and the horrible reality in *Modern Times*.

In *The Dictator* he plays the two opposite poles of infantilism—the victor and the vanquished.

The line of the Mexican border in *The Pilgrim* seems to have cut Chaplin in two: one half is Hynkel, the other—the little barber.

Perhaps that is the reason why this film is so impressive.

And perhaps that is why it is in this film that Chaplin speaks for the first time.

Because for the first time he is not a slave of his method and his way of seeing things; for the first time he has taken the method and purposeful exposition into his hands, the hands of a grown-up man.

And this, in its turn, is due to the fact that it is the first time that we hear the distinct, clear and convincing voice of the civic courage of not merely a grown-up man, but of a Great Man, of a really great man.

Perhaps this is achieved through the image of a ridiculous, shuffling little man, but here Chaplin voices his condemnation of fascism like a grown-up, mature person, in a majestic and perfectly convincing manner.

It is not *his attitude* to this pest of humanity that is infantile in this film; for the first time it is only *the method of voicing* his scathing condemnation, the foundation of his attitude, that is infantile.

The appeal in the finale of *The Dictator* may be considered symbolic of the process showing Charlie the kid growing into Charlie the impassionate tribune.

In an interview about *Modern Times* Chaplin said that many thought the film propagandistic, but it was only a burlesque on the universal confusion which brought suffering to all. He added that the film would not have been entertaining if he had tried to tell the public what to do about it. In that case, he said, it would have been necessary to do it seriously from an orator's platform.

And he used the finale of *The Dictator* as a platform.

The author of *The Dictator* has become a tribune of the people, advocating at anti-fascist meetings the only measure humanity must take—to destroy fascism.

I started writing my notes on Chaplin way back in 1937.

There was no *Dictator* at that time.

Its target—the obnoxious visage of fascism—was just beginning to stretch its greedy, blood-stained tentacles towards Europe out of the filth and blood in its own country.

In that same year I dropped the idea of writing about Chaplin—I just didn't know how to round out the article. It is clear to me now that what I needed then to give a proper image of Chaplin the man and artist was a film like *The Dictator*.

Today we are fighting fascism waist-deep in blood.

And today finds us side by side, friends and comrades-at-arms, with Chaplin, fighting against humanity's common enemy.

In this fight we need not only bayonets and bullets, aeroplanes and tanks, grenades and minethrowers but also the inspired word, the powerful image of a work of art, the passionate temperament of an artist and satirist who can kill with ridicule.

And today—
it is Charlie,
it is Chaplin,
who,
by one method or other,
by some means or other,
in one way or other,
looking at life with his childishly naïve and *childishly wise* eyes,
creates in *The Dictator* an impressive and devastating satire glorifying the Triumph of the Human Mind over Bestiality.

Thereby Chaplin takes his place in the ranks of the great masters who, throughout the ages, have been fighting Darkness with the weapon of Satire—he takes his place beside Aristophanes of Athens, Erasmus of Rotterdam, François Rabelais of Meudon, Jonathan Swift of Dublin, François Marie Arouet Voltaire of Ferney.

Perhaps his place is in front of them if we take into consideration the magnitude of the fascist Goliath of Baseness, Crime and Obscurantism, who is reeling under the blows of ridicule from the youngest of the Davids—
Charles Spencer Chaplin of Hollywood,
known henceforward as *Charlie the Grown-Up.*

1943-44

HELLO, CHARLIE!

In these days of your jubilee I recollect with particular pleasure the six months in Hollywood during which we met, played tennis, cruised in your yacht off Catalina Island in the Pacific and visited popular resorts, where boys slapped you on the back with a friendly "Hello, Charlie!"

It was not only in our works of art that you were interested in those years. You were displaying increasing interest in the Soviet Union, which was producing such surprisingly unusual—for you—motion pictures.

That autumn (1930) you were filming *City Lights*. At that time you saw the world divided into "good" and "bad" people. It seemed a mere accident that the "bad" people were on one side of the social barrier and the "good" on the other. But your growing interest in the first socialist state in the world was gradually opening your eyes. And the abstract categories of good and evil, of good and bad people, were taking on a class meaning. *Modern Times* shows your first steps in that direction.

Rampant fascist aggression, the brutality of fascism as it trampled underfoot all human ideals could not fail to arouse the indignation of such a splendid and humane artist as you are. Judging from what we hear about you from afar, you are approaching closer and closer what we Soviet artists consider the ultimate goal of our activities, of our work, of our life—the active fight for the great ideals of justice and humanism.

There can be no honest man, to say nothing of artist, and especially one as splendid as you are, who, in these times of terrible fascist obscurantism, can remain indifferent to the bright ideal of humanity realized on one-sixth of the globe.

Each serves this ideal in his own way.

Yours has been the way of art, so beloved of all the world because of the ardent advocacy of humanism by which your films have been distinguished from the outstart.

For your love of man, for your striving to participate in mankind's struggle for human dignity and an existence worthy of man, for your beautiful art I would like to slap you on the back—the way you Americans express your esteem of one another—and say from the bottom of my heart: "Hello, Chaplin! May we walk arm in arm for many years to come, fighting for the finest human ideals!"

May this greeting fly to you across the seas and oceans, across the blood-black patches of fascist states marring the face of the earth, that lie between us.

Forward together with us, for the great ideals which are being realized in our country!

1939

THE DICTATOR

A Charlie Chaplin Film

1. BLACK BUTTERFLY

Fate in its irony has made the black butterfly of identical moustache settle on the upper lip of two completely different men. One of them is an invention, a mask. The other is real flesh and blood. The former is one of the most popular men on the globe. The latter is positively the most hated.

"He stole my moustache!" Charlie clamoured merrily in newspapers, accusing Hitler of plagiarism. "It was I who invented it!"

Hitler seemed nothing more than a comedian, a buffoon, and Chaplin's accusation that he had stolen his make-up made Hitler look like a clown.

But as the years went on it became clear that Hitler was something more than a comedian, buffoon and clown; he proved to be a homicidal maniac.

And Chaplin made his *Dictator.*

2 WHAT IS THE FILM ABOUT?

A fascist dictator has a double: a little Ghetto barber. Chaplin plays both.

...The sign of the Double-Cross overshadows the enslaved Tomania. The tramp of heavy marching boots resounds in its streets night and day. At night, the brutal faces of storm-troopers peer out of every corner.

The words heard oftenest are: "storm detachments," "concentration camps," "dictator."

A palace on a distant mountain is occupied by Hynkel, the dictator of Tomania, the most hated man in the world. A madman who thinks his mission is to conquer the world, who dreams of becoming the lord of the universe in which there will be only Aryans.

The only person unaware of the changes around him is the little barber, who has been long absent from the Ghetto. It is many years since he was shell-shocked in the First World War and he spent them in a distant hospital. One day he decided he had had enough of it, slipped away and returned home.

Gaily he sets about putting in order his modest barber-shop: removes the cobwebs, cleans the dust off the ledger and begins carefully to remove the streaks of white paint somebody had smeared over his shop, without noticing that they spell the word *Jude*.

The injudicious actions of the little barber are observed by the watchdogs of the Double-Cross who raid the long-suffering Ghetto in reprisal. Among those who suffer at the hands of the raiders is that nice old man, Mr. Jeckel. And his wife. And the charming little washerwoman Hanna (Paulette Goddard) who launders the linen for the entire neighbourhood....

...The Ghetto recovers from the blow. The little barber screws up enough courage to invite the little washerwoman for a walk one Sunday, and the whole Ghetto comes out into the streets to see him walk by her side, swinging his cane with a proud and independent air. Scarcely do they take a few steps when they are rooted to the spot by the Dictator's frenzied screams coming over the loud speaker and portending death and destruction. A new raid. The storm-troopers are looking for the little barber who has dared resist the Dictator.

Little Hanna hides him on a house roof. But he is found. A short pursuit and he is in a concentration camp.

The barber escapes with a friend, Schultz, who was once a member of the Dictator's headquarters but who was sent to the camp for telling the truth to his face.

Schultz is the first to notice the striking resemblance between the Dictator and the little barber.

Their height, figures, faces, including the black butterfly of a moustache, are identical. But even Schultz did not expect what happens when they reach Austerlich (Austria) after their escape. They do not know that the Dictator has just annexed Austerlich and is expected there.

The little barber is taken for the Dictator. He is dragged before a multitude of microphones and made to speak.

3. TWO SPEECHES

From the screen comes the second speech, so significant for this significant film. The first speech Chaplin delivers as Hynkel. It was one of those famous Chaplin speeches, the first outlines of which are given in the address at the unveiling of the monument in *City Lights* and in the verses in *Modern Times*. Without words, without meaning, a torrent of inarticulate cries, howls and screams perfectly expressing the senselessness, demagogy and hysteria of the speeches of the world's greatest demagogue and criminal, whose name will always symbolize blood-thirstiness, cruelty, obscurantism and violence.

In reply to this oration of Hynkel's comes the speech of the little barber, mistaken for the Dictator.

The little barber, his shyness disappearing, says his say before the multitude of microphones and crowds of people.

He has overcome his fright and irresoluteness, and the microphones carry his voice far away. This is the voice of all the oppressed nations wherever they may be suffering under the bestial yoke of fascism.

Far, far away are Hanna and his friends of the Ghetto, horrified at the darkness and the fate awaiting them. The little barber's words to her are a call to all who rise to fight fascism in the name of humanity. "...Courage, Hanna! Courage, for hope is not dead.... Somewhere the sun will rise again for you, for us, for all who suffer on this earth.... Humanity will not be beaten!"

4. THE MOST IMPORTANT THING

It is noteworthy that it is in this vein, in this key that the newspapers and magazines in America write about this film.

It is of this that press notices and articles speak.

Somewhere in the background are the ecstasies at the satirical characterizations of Hynkel with the Double-Cross and of Napaloni with dice on his tasselled black cap. Somewhere deep in the background is the description of the comedy gags.

They notice in passing that the military episodes seem to have come from the old film *Shoulder Arms*, they chuckle over the scene showing the two dictators in the barbers' chairs, they mention the technique of Chaplin's break-neck fall through the glass roof and several floors.

But I repeat that this time it is not such and similar details that strike those who write about the film.

Hatred of the fascist oppressors is what fills the hearts of those who see the picture. The episode with the obliterated inscription seems to obliterate the particular nature of the events in the Ghetto, substituting for them the fate of entire small countries and nations languishing under fascism, no matter whether the country is called Belgium, Norway, Greece, Holland, Yugoslavia, France or Czechoslovakia.

5. SPEAKING ALOUD

The last "trick" in this film is that for the first time Chaplin speaks in his own voice: he voices the indictment in his own words, in his own person.

Formalists and aesthetes dare reproach him with this: to them the structure of a film is more important than a live human appeal.

But that does not daunt Chaplin. He has been filling his lungs with the air of social protest from one film to another.

In his short comedies and in *The Kid* the protest was against the division of the world into "good" and "bad" people. The bloody nightmare of fascism made Chaplin raise his voice against this abominable product of capitalist reaction, against fascism. And at this moment from Chaplin's silent and musical screen comes his human and humane voice.

The American magazine *Friday* is right in saying that Adolf Hitler has millions of enemies but that one of the most formidable foes of the *Führer* is a little man born in the same year with him—Charlie Chaplin.

6. SOMEWHERE THE SUN WILL RISE AGAIN

These hopeful words of the little barber have come true. The little barber can rest assured:

Fascism will be destroyed!

1941

ALWAYS FORWARD

(BY WAY OF AN EPILOGUE)

You mustn't read other people's letters. That's what we are taught as children.

But there are other people's letters through which I like to leaf now and then, which I read, which I swallow with avidity.

These are the letters of painters.

The letters of Serov.

The letters of Michelangelo.

There the molten mass of words twists and turns as passionately and convulsively as do his monumental *slaves* tearing themselves away from the unfinished stone slabs, as do his sinners hurled into Hell, as do the sleeping figures on the Medici tombs, oppressed by morbid dreams.

Some letters moan.

Moans fill the pages of the letters he wrote at the time he was decorating the vaults of the Sistine Chapel.

Months and months spent in an unnaturally bent position. With head thrown back. With arms benumbed. With legs filled with lead.

With plaster falling into inflamed eyes.

With tools falling from hands.

With head swimming.

With scaffolding swaying to and fro and nailing the flight of creative imagination to the ruthlessly immovable surface of the ceiling.

But the months of suffering are past.

The scaffolding is dismantled.

The benumbed limbs are stretched.

The bent back is straightened.

The head is raised proudly.

The creator looks up.

The creator contemplates his work.

The vaults give way before him.

The stone gives way to heaven.

These frescoes seem to be the summit of the triumph of the human spirit born anew in those new times, the goal of the best of the Renaissance artists.

Some narrow-minded people ask:

"Where can you find paintings and statues to compare with the creations of the giants of the Renaissance?"

"Where can one find a forest of statues belonging to a more advanced era to take the place of *David*?"

"Where are the frescoes to outshine *The Lord's Supper*?"

"Where are the canvases to eclipse the *Sistine Madonna*?"

"Is there no more strength left in the creative spirit of nations? Has the creative will of mankind lost its power?"

"Where must we look for monuments of human endeavour to represent an age as Parthenon represents the florescence of Greece, Gothic architecture the Middle Ages and the giants of the Renaissance—their epoch?"

To my mind, our epoch will preserve its personality in an art which is as far removed from the fresco as the skyscraper is from the basilica; an art as far removed from stained-glass window as the jet plane is from the boldest plans of Leonardo da Vinci; an art it is as impossible to compare with the chisel of Benvenuto Cellini as it is impossible to compare the destructive action of Borgia's poisons with that of the atomic bomb, or the intuition of Brunelleschi with the precise calculation based on the formulas of present-day scientists. The very nature of new works of art will make them incommensurable with the works of past epochs, just as there can be no comparison between the epoch which, in the twentieth century, produced the Land of Socialism, and the earlier epochs.

The inner essence, too, will make this art incommensurable with the art of the past, for it will not be new music versus old, a new painting art vying with the old, a new theatre striving to outstrip the old, not drama, sculpture, dancing emerging victorious from competition with the arts of the past.

It will be a wonderful new art merging in a unified whole, presenting a synthesis of painting and drama, music and sculpture, architecture and dancing, landscape and man, visual image and uttered word.

Recognition of this synthesis as an organic unity non-existent before is certainly the most important achievement in the history of aesthetics.

This new art is the cinema.

The early and elementary forms of such synthesis were known to the Greeks at the dawn of culture.

There have been many dreamers advocating new forms in the realization of this ideal.

This was advocated at different times by Diderot, Wagner and Scriabin.

The times were different. And yet they had one trait in common.

Those were the times not yet aroused by the clarion call demanding an end to the exploitation of one part of humanity by another, to the enslavement of nations by colonizers, to the oppression of people by their conquerors.

In those days there was no country on earth where this was not a dream but reality, not a theory but practice, not a mirage but actual life.

So it was quite natural that from the very first days of the existence of our wonderful country our leaders pointed out in no uncertain terms that the cinema was the most important of arts. And it was as natural that those engaged in this most important of arts considered it from the start the most progressive of arts, an art worthy of giving expression to the era of the Victorious Socialist Revolution, an art capable of perfectly embodying the image of the new man.

The ways and means of this new art cannot be compared with anything in the past. And the same applies to its new and unusual methods.

It is not the result of the labour of hundreds of thousands of stone-masons, sculptors and builders, who erected breath-takingly beautiful cathedrals but whose names are lost.

It is collaboration of strongly marked talents and individualities of equal standing, each with his own characteristic handwriting working in the sphere of sound, histrionics, photography, costume, acoustics, photographic processing, laboratory and direction.

In their spirit the films express the ideas of millions (otherwise would millions go to see them?), they embody the principle of collectivism and cooperation characteristic of the era of democracy.

In this team-work it is not a lone Michelangelo that spends months on his scaffolding.

It takes scores, nay, hundreds of people to produce a film. One is busy with blueprints and calculations. Another selects the required shades from the spectrum of innumerable shades of filters. A third intently analyzes and searches for the most expressive among the simultaneously run sound tracks. And a fourth looks for their equivalent in the plastic succession of shots.

And thus all through the ten, twenty, forty, fifty years of that difficult and incomparably joyous work known as film creation.

Let us, like Michelangelo, straighten our collective back, take our eyes off laboratory vessels, colour filters and cans, from flood-lights, props, written parts and scores.

Let us raise our eyes to the vaults above. What do we see?

Just as in the boundless heavens of the immortal frescoes which took the place of what but a short time ago had been a stone vault, the eye sees boundless new prospects and possibilities.

Just as in the frescoes the old Adam gave way to the new Adam, the man of the Renaissance, so here, too, we see the as yet not fully developed picture of cinematography's new potentialities.

Our heads swim as we throw them back to look into the future.

We seem to be standing on the vertex of the pyramid built during the half century of the history of our art.

It has vast and numerous achievements to its credit.

Its base is broad and spacious.

Its sides rise steeply upwards.

Its vertex rises proudly into the sky.

But as we gaze up, it seems that from the vertex, as from a new zero point, there grows in all four directions a new giant with sides capable of embracing the impetuously growing boundaries of imagination. It is the immense image of the new consciousness and world closing upon us which our cinema is called on to reflect.

And can we say that the screen itself is not dissolving before our eyes in the newest achievements of the stereoscopic film, projecting representations not only onto a wall but throughout the entire auditorium, taking it along in its swift race into the boundless space around us through the magic of television?

Can we say that this explosion within the very nature and essence of our idea of entertainment is not natural? It is brought about by the development of technology precisely at a moment when a new aesthetic system, born in the new stage of the development of society, is expecting new feats of it. This stage of social development has at its disposal the necessary new instruments for controlling nature and working changes in human consciousness equal to those which occurred at the dawn of culture when man made the first working tool.

Will not the new art which appeared in the process of man's conquest of nature with these new instruments of unheard-of potency throw its light on the heaven as a fore-runner of those new forms of consciousness?

. . . .

We must develop conciousness to enable it to fulfil these new tasks.

We must sharpen the pointed edge of our thoughts to solve these tasks.

We must master past experience in the interests of the future.
We must work tirelessly.
We must seek incessantly.
We must face boldly the new era in art.
We must work, work and work—
in the name of an art born to spread the greatest ideas of our era
among the millions.

1947

DRAWINGS
DIRECTOR'S CROQUIS
AND SKETCHES

"The author sees with his mind's eye some image, an emotional embodiment of his theme. His task is to reduce that image to two or three *partial representations* whose combination or juxtaposition shall evoke in the consciousness and feelings of the spectator the same generalized initial image which haunted the author's imagination." These words of Sergei Eisenstein's may well be used as an epigraph to his drawings.

Eisenstein not only elaborated in detail the appearance of all the characters in his films, their make-up, costumes, gestures and motions, but drew pictures of almost all the important sequences and shots. His drawings for *Alexander Nevsky* or *Ivan the Terrible*, for instance, show that he had a perfect knowledge of the epoch he was filming—more, that ancient Russian architecture was near to him and that he felt at home in low-vaulted refectories and cathedrals, that the time-darkened frescoes were for him not inanimate museum pieces but the animated scene of astonishingly dynamic action.

This is what Eisenstein wrote of his drawings for the films:

"Without seeing the characters moving and acting, without seeing the *mises-en-scène*, it is impossible to note all this on paper. They are in constant motion before my eyes. Sometimes I see them so plainly I believe I could draw them with my eyes closed ... that is how my drawings appear. They are not illustrations to the script ... sometimes they express the essence of the feeling the scene is to arouse, and more often—searchings.

"They are pictorial shorthand notes and lay no claim to anything else."

Eisenstein could portray equally well highly tragic and comic situations, stationariness and dynamics, the exalted heroism of Alexander Nevsky and flippant polka-grotesque, the fantastic flight of the Valkyries and the eyes of a Mexican youth full of sorrow and wrath, a funny self-caricature and the sinister image of Richard III. He often portrayed generalized images— those of Ibsen and Maeterlinck, of Tragedy, of Ballet, of the Clown, the Juggler . . . .

senstein's   caricature   of
nself

Early sketch

Polka-Grotesque

Sketch for the ballet *Queen of Spades* (it was never staged)

ТРАГЕДИЯ

Tragedy

The Juggler

Ballet

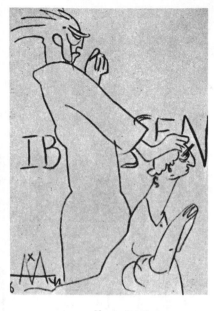

Ibsen

Maeterlinck

Daumier

A Mexican sketch. To the market-place

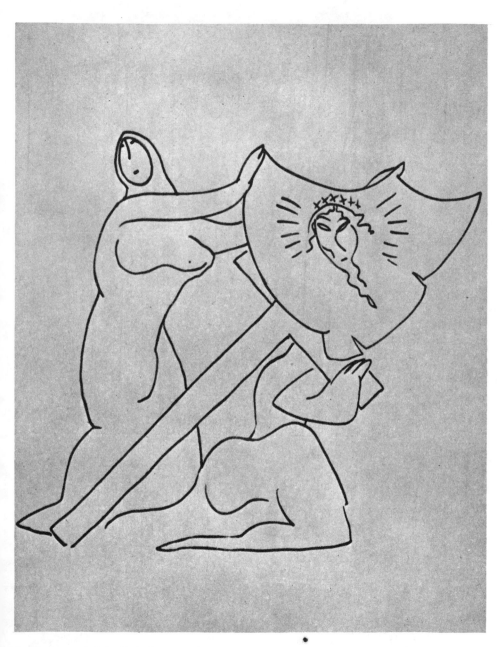

A Mexican sketch. Religious ecstasy

Mexican peon

Mexican youth

Mexicans

Sketches of characters for *Alexander Nevsky*

Sketch of the opening shot of *Alexander Nevsky*

Gavrilo and Buslai (*Alexander Nevsky*)

A monk blesses the Teuton knights before the battle
(*Alexander Nevsky*)

Sketch of the Battle on the Ice

The meeting between Buslai and Gavrilo

Sketch of a shot (*Alexander Nevsky*)

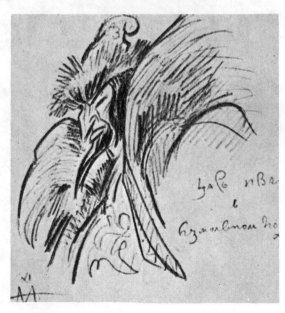

Sketches of Tsar Ivan's head
(*Ivan the Terrible*)

The capture of Kazan. Tsar Ivan at twilight

Tsar Ivan and Kurbsky (*Ivan the Terrible*)

The capture of Kazan

Death of Yelena Glinskaya, the Tsar's mother (*Ivan the Terrible*)

Тяжелым бредом присутствующе
свободит царь Иван

The ailing Tsar

Death of Anastasya, the Tsar's wife

КТО ВЗЫВАЕТ КО ГОСПОДИ?

Ivan's penance

Religious procession in Alexandrova Sloboda
(*Ivan the Terrible*)

Religious procession in Alexandrova Sloboda
(*Ivan the Terrible*)

Prince Andrei Shuisky (*Ivan the Terrible*)